THE GOD THEORY

By
Ronald Lewis Tarter

PublishAmerica

Baltimore

First printing

ISBN: 1-59129-380-4
PUBLISHED BY PUBLISHAMERICA BOOK
PUBLISHERS
www.publishamerica.com
Baltimore

Printed in the United States of America

DEDICATION

Authors traditionally dedicate books to wives, children, parents, friends and people whom they admire. While I appreciate the tolerance of my wife and children during this seemingly endless project, and the sacrifices of my parents in raising me, this dedication must go to the forces of moderation and open-mindedness around our globe—to men and women of all colors, ethnicities and religious backgrounds who are locked in a perpetual struggle against the twin forces of repression and ignorance. In my own personal careers (as a planner and an adjunct professor), spanning nearly 30 years, I have often had occasion to witness the marvelous ability of science to promote reason and point in the direction of human progress. We cannot afford to bend to the will of zealots who would ignore the lessons of history and return us to the "dark ages." Science must continue to be a great guiding light for progress, and a logical platform from which we can address even the greatest mysteries of the universe.

THE GOD THEORY:
INTRODUCTION

"In the beginning God created the heavens and the earth."
(Genesis 1:1)[1]

Do you believe it? If so, you are not alone! The God called "Yahweh" by Jews, "Jehovah" by Christians, and "Allah" by Moslems is worshiped by three billion people—roughly forty-five percent of the world's population. He is authoritatively described by Genesis as the Creator of the universe, and as One Who brought all of creation into being within a timespan of only six days. Yet, the cumulative findings of science over the past four centuries would *seem* to challenge the credibility of Genesis, suggesting that the universe physically *evolved* into its current state-of-being across billions of years. Rigid and ultra-conservative scriptural interpretations render the prevailing messages of Genesis and science irreconcilable. However, liberal, non-literal approaches tend to square the primary tenets of Genesis with those of science. *The God Theory* is a product of the latter approach. Its purpose, in part, is to show that science and scripture *are* reconcilable when scriptures are interpreted in their proper context, and when the errors and bad science of antiquity are purged from theology. *The God Theory* builds a broad philosophical platform for interweaving science and theology—from which we can expand our knowledge of the universe and better comprehend the nature of God and eternity.

Early in the 20th Century, physicists believed that subatomic *particles* formed the smallest and most fundamental units of nature. As the century progressed, it was found that subatomic particles were themselves composed of smaller sub-particles called quarks. Then, late in the 20th Century, an innovative new theory emerged suggesting that *all* particles and sub-particles are formed from *"cosmic strings"* and that cosmic strings constitute the smallest and most fundamental units of nature—perhaps interlinking the entire universe. *In short, new theories and findings have dramatically altered our perception of the universe over the last 100 years. Theology and the philosophical disciplines are still adjusting to those changes.*

The new and rapidly increasing power of science has adequately equipped it for speculation about the greatest of all mysteries, including even the nature of God and eternity. While one can go too far in trying to synchronize science and scripture, *The God Theory* will demonstrate that important new windows on the universe can be gained by thoughtful, meticulous interweaving of *correlative* scientific and scriptural information. The notion of a grand scientific and scriptural composite is by no means new. Two centuries ago, scientists and theologians shared a common belief that science *opens* the scriptures to improved comprehension. Theologians studied nature in order to learn more about God. Today, however, scientists and theologians have been driven into opposing camps by uncompromising atheists and fundamentalists—by people who insist that science and scripture are irreconcilable and that they should have nothing to do with each other.

During the 20th Century, findings in astronomy and physics essentially proved beyond doubt that the universe is one, and this greatly undermines the arguments of "irreconcilers." In a truly *"Divine Creation"* how is it possible for scriptures (created by God) not to square with a natural world (created by God)? A rational and intelligent God Who created everything, and Who gave us a mind to ultimately comprehend the scriptures would also have placed in the scriptures the correct and proper version of creation. A rational and caring God, out of respect for Himself and His creation, would not **make** a world of obvious laws and realities and then *tell us* (in Holy Scriptures) something radically opposed to those laws and realities. The Bible, itself, asserts that such a contradiction is impossible. The

Book of Psalms testifies to the pervasive harmony between God and nature, and to the fact that God is integral to nature. Psalms 19:1 states that: "The heavens declare the glory of God, and the firmament showeth His handiwork." Deuteronomy asserts that pronouncements which are truly the Word of God always come true, and that those which turn out to be false are not of God. Science has a similar perspective—eloquently versed by the late, great physicist, Richard Feynmann—that the only real truth stems from that which we can observe and measure in the real world.

Such ideas converge and suggest that if God truly exists, we should somehow be able to find physical evidence of Him in nature. *The God Theory* will sustain this notion, but it will not sustain a fundamental premise of 2nd Century *Gnostics* that knowledge is the *key* to salvation. *The God Theory* is not a defense of gnosticism. It is, however, a defense of our need to search for God, and our inherent right to use the power of science in trying to find Him. More than anything else, it stresses our growing need to use science in interpreting scripture and our concurrent need to update theology.

Scientists often espouse the *oneness* of the universe, and basic ties between science and scripture. However, change is a constant in science, and reactionary groups always find change threatening. Historically, religious extremists have been among the most predisposed to suppress the truth by force. We need only take a brief look around to determine that this is still the case, that supression is still with us, and that the present is not so very different from the past:

> ...Then came a time near the beginning of the seventeenth century when science and mathematics began to take hold of men's minds, to stir imaginations, and to invoke new theories, new experiments... Ideas were being promulgated that high church officials had neither the time, the knowledge, nor the inclination to absorb and evaluate. Scientific findings seemed to conflict with literal scriptural interpretations, and as

such were unacceptable. The church felt called upon to defend its own presentation of the Word of God and to discipline this new breed of dissenter.

We can look back smugly now and wonder how such a thing could ever have happened. Yet if we don't look back at all but just look around, we find similar situations existing today, but now it's not the Roman Catholics. Protestant fundamentalists operate colleges awarding advanced degrees, including a doctoral degree in creation science, for the study of a literal interpretation of the biblical Book of Genesis that proves the world is not much over four thousand years old. Accordingly, creation science rejects the modern teachings of geology, anthropology, paleontology, archaeology and linguistics, and scoffs at the practice of carbon dating.

In 1987, in a town near my home in Kentucky, the local newspaper reported that members of the county school board had called on an elementary school teacher at her home. She was told that if she ever again dared to repeat the sin she had committed that week, it could mean her discharge from the school. Her sin? She had shown children a National Geographic film about dinosaurs that spoke of an earth millions of years old, in direct violation of the revealed Word of God...[2]

The Galileo Inquisition of 1633 should be required reading for all biblical literalists and for those otherwise fearful of science. About 20 years prior to his arrest, Galileo had published a study confirming the *Copernican sun-centered model of the universe*. His findings openly flew in the face of a sacrosanct Church doctrine favoring the *"Ptolemaic earth-centered model," which had become a centerpiece* of Christian doctrine during the first and second centuries A.D. The Ptolemaic model had evolved into a complex assemblage of dogma. Contrary to popular impressions, it embraced far more than the simple notion that the Earth was at the center of the universe. In many respects, its central idea was that of *a universe composed of "spheres-within-spheres."*

The Ptolemaic model held that the *sphere of the Earth* lay at the center of creation. This sphere was thought to be surrounded by and encased within a larger, outlying *sphere of the "heavenly waters."* The sphere of heavenly waters, in turn, was said to be encased within other outlying, progressively larger spheres containing the sun and moon, the planets, the stars, and finally heaven, itself. While this was a model rooted in ancient Sumerian/Middle-Eastern astronomy, its credibility in the eyes of medieval clerics lay in the fact that it was sustained by none other than a literal interpretation of Genesis!

The first chapter of Genesis describes a *"firmament"* created by God, separating the (oceanic) **waters** of the Earth **from** the (heavenly) **waters** surrounding the Earth. It relates God to that environment, noting that He moved *"across the face of the (heavenly) waters"* prior to the onset of the creation process. Later, the seventh chapter of Genesis reports that the *"fountains of the great deep"* were broken open, and the passage of these fountains (i.e. waters) through the rent firmament separating heavenly and oceanic waters becomes the cause of the great deluge that we have termed "Noah's flood." Indeed, numerous examples can be extracted from Genesis making it abundantly clear that geocentrism and discrete heavenly spheres, i.e. the primary tenets of the Ptolemaic model, are nothing more or less than *biblical.*

But is God truly the source of such absurd notions? History shows that the Ptolemaic model was not *simply* a theological creation. Like much of our modern theological heritage, secular thought and archaic tradition lay at its basis. In the ancient world, deprived as it was of the tools of modern astronomy, *geocentrism seemed perfectly consistent with reality—almost common-sensical.* Anyone standing on the Earth's surface, observing the heavens, could clearly see the sun, moon and stars to be in constant motion across the sky. These heavenly bodies seemed to move while the Earth seemed to remain stationary. Ancient astronomers perceived not the fact that the Earth's movement was only creating *an illusion that the heavens were moving*. Since geocentric notions appear in Chinese and Sumerian records dating as far back as 30 or 40 centuries ago, the notion of geocentrism is as old as the discipline of astronomy, and seems to extend back to the very dawn of human civilization. In Chapter One I will show that biblical geocentrism is linked to such ancient secular beliefs, and that it is a human creation, and not, by any means, part of a Divine Revelation. The clerics who persecuted Galileo, however, knew only the teachings of their predecessors and the *literal* words of Genesis. By weight of literalism, church tradition and peer pressure, they had come to believe that the idea was Divine in origin. Without tacit understanding of the cultural/historical roots of the Ptolemaic Model, they simply read its inclusion in scripture as a Divine edict and endorsement. For a millennium and a half prior to the time of Galileo, the Church had heaped pile upon pile of dogma onto this crazy notion. Clerics came to see God as *an outsider*, a supernatural observer Who resided somewhere "above the clouds," "in the sky," and/or out "beyond the firmament of the heavens" (views which are still very much with us).

*Believing that God resided in the outermost of the heavenly spheres, the leaders of the early church had also created the notion of a gradation of perfection between a **totally perfect heaven** out along the periphery of everything, and **a highly imperfect Earth** at the center of it all. After Magellan proved that the world was round, it became common belief that hell—the very height of imperfection— lay at the exact center of the Earth (i.e. the exact center of the universe)*. The sun, moon, planets, stars, and *anything substantially beyond the Earth*, by contrast, were thought to belong to increasingly perfect realms of the universe. So it was that when Galileo published evidence of pits and craters on the Moon (showing imperfection and decay), he flew in the face of all that had become sacred.

Most importantly, his assertions directly undermined the authority of the Church. Notions of celestial perfection had been incorporated by Rome into an even larger doctrine of a grand scheme of things that served God. Clerics believed that God dispatched angels, each day, to *physically move* the sun, moon, planets and stars across the sky. These angels willingly served God and obeyed His commands. Similarly, God had created all of the creatures and beasts of the Earth to serve man, *and man, himself, was to serve God by obedience to the ecclesiastical hierarchy of the Church.* The entire universe was therefore seen to be a place of Divinely-instilled moral and physical *order, with all components of the universe ordered to the service of God.* This being the case, it was impossible even to consider that the model might have originated in an archaic, godless, pagan society.

In announcing his findings, Galileo implicitly attacked the geocentric model and the notion of Divine perfection, and brought down the entire deck of cards. Without geocentrism and a gradation of perfection, there could be no "divine order," and therefore no justification for obedience to *the church as the agent of God on Earth.* Having published such a threatening treatise, Galileo quickly found himself playing hardball with the Pope, and using a very thin glove! Criticism and intimidation followed, then arrest, trial, and threats of imprisonment and torture. Ultimately, he was forced to recant his observations and to be confined to house arrest for the remainder of his life. A few decades after his death, however, the Dutch astronomer Huygens—a resident of protestant Holland, and safely outside the realm of influence of the pope—proved the Copernican Model (and Galileo) correct beyond all doubt. The rest, it seems, is history.

Today, no one considers the notion of a tiny, spherical Earth-centered universe to be credible. *However, powerful cultural and theological forces have **inflicted** a biblical interpretation on us that still supports the geocentric model. The hard-line, literalistic interpretation of Genesis inherently ends up embracing this model, and the same sort of God who ruled that archaic, nonsensical universe!* **In disproving the Ptolemaic model, what Galileo and Huygens ultimately disproved was the validity of a literal interpretation of Genesis. This cast great doubt upon literalism as a device for reliably interpreting the scriptures.**

There are two alternatives for dealing with this dilemma, either: (1) accept a premise that the Bible is incorrect, invalid and totally worthless, or (2) accept a premise that the Bible is a product of human culture and history *as well as (perhaps) Divine Revelation. If the second alternative is correct, then it is possible to contend that biblical errors result from human rather than divine input, and that there is an innate need to separate between the human inputs and those that are innately divine.* Thus, **only by refuting doctrines of biblical inerrancy, can a person with knowledge of history, science, and the saga of scientists such as Copernicus and Galileo, accept a notion that portions of the Bible may, in fact, contain true Divine Revelation.** Only by accepting the fact that the Bible contains history, culture and politics—in addition to (perhaps) Divine Revelation—can a person of knowledge accept it at all.

Moslems argue that the Judeo-Christian Bible has been corrupted. Whether this is true, or not, is an issue for another book, but it is something that we must be concerned with. In Chapter One I will argue that the Ptolemaic model was, in fact, transfused into the Hebrew scriptures from secular, pagan sources during the Babylonian captivity, and that its source was certainly not Divine. After Babylon fell to the Persians, scriptures that had been extensively revised and rewritten by Jewish priests during the Babylonian captivity were carried back to Palestine, and subsequently made their way into the Jewish communities of northern Egypt. Thereupon, history records that during the Second Century B.C., these "Septuagint" scriptures were incorporated into the Great Library of Alexandria, in northern Egypt. *History also records that more than 300 years later, around A.D. 150, Claudius Prolemaeus, the most famous of the librarians of Alexandria, altered the prevailing version of the geocentric model to incorporate the notion of perfect geometric precision (which was later to plague Galileo), and Prolemaeus probably either directly or indirectly convinced the Greek King Ptolemy I of its validity. It was Ptolemy, in turn, who convinced the early Christian church that geocentrism was deserving of doctrinal status.*

The entire "Septuagint" was ultimately incorporated into Christian scriptures without question, and thus became accepted by the early Church. In Chapter One, we will see in more detail how the geocentric model tacitly embraced by the Septuagint (and medieval theologians) conflicted with the findings of Copernicus, Galileo and Huygens, and how these men ultimately *proved that the Bible (as commonly interpreted then and now) is not error-free*. Over the past 400 years, of course, a great many theologians have conveniently ignored that fact. Obviously, it is easier for nonbelievers to accept Christianity or Judaism if the entire Bible is seen as divine. If only part of the Bible is divine, then which part is it? And how do we know which part to keep and which part to throw out? This is ultimately a nightmarish issue for theologians, but as we shall see in later chapters, some resolution of this issue can be achieved via the formulation of scientific-scriptural composites—and by establishment of proper biblical context. The scriptures repeatedly assert that God is perfect, and a truly *perfect God cannot possibly be the author of error!* Therefore, biblical errors, such as they are, can only be laid at the feet of human beings. Frankly, I want the reader to remember this as he/she proceeds through this book, because I'm not attacking the Bible, I'm attacking its revisions and interpretations. Biblical geocentrism is obviously erroneous and therefore could not have been placed there by a perfect God. By the same token, other pronouncements that are in the Bible and erroneous cannot be laid at the doorstep of The Almighty. The facts, overall, suggest that the Bible contains artifacts of human history, culture and politics, and that these are altogether distinct and separate from the Word of God. To teach that the entire Bible is literally and pervasively true and divine therefore mocks that which is *truly* of God, and does it a disservice.

Theology cannot survive the new millennium upon a cornerstone of error. Recognizing this, it is my belief that the prevailing image of God and Creation must be reshaped so that it appropriately interfaces with truths that can be observed in the universe through science. The *God Theory* is in part a conceptual basis for reshaping modern theology, and I hope that it can be used by our descendants to attune the divine to the natural universe, and separate the divine from the human.

This book arrives 400 years too late to preserve the authority of the Church, and 400 years too late to head-off the great wave of reaction against all forms of religion set in motion by the Galileo fiasco. Theologians can only learn from their mistakes, not reverse the damage that has already been done. At the same time, the long march of human history indicates that God is an adept counter-puncher Who may be deftly using our mistakes to achieve His goals. The reaction against the church that followed the Galileo Inquisition is the root of our current scientific, political and religious freedoms, *and ultimately the basis of the "God Theory," and similar genre.* After Huygens, atheists spilled out of the closet and assumed leadership roles in science and politics. In the resulting Era of Rationalism, the influence of the Church waned, suppression of new ideas became impossible, and the world opened to a new age of discovery and change.

The next three centuries formed an epoch like nothing seen before or since. Charles Lyell stepped forward with the discipline of Geology and showed that the Earth was very old, and that its landforms had been produced by slow and gradualistic changes, rather than by quick, catastrophic events like "Noah's Flood." Linnaeus added a system of biological classification that allowed scientists to effectively inter-relate species. Then along came Charles Darwin, who stepped onto the shoulders of Lyell and Linnaeus with a new theory of evolution suggesting that the Earth's biota had slowly evolved into being from simpler species. Mendel followed with "genetics," and tied inherited characteristics of living creatures to fundamental attributes (genes) carried by individual cells. Finally, during the 19th Century, optical improvements led to more powerful telescopes, and astronomers suddenly had an ability to view the heavens in great detail. As man gained the ability to gauge himself in terms of the entire observable universe, new ideas began to spring up about the origin of the universe—ideas based on scientific observation that had been formed independently of religious influence.

The "Steady State Theory," formulated by Sir James Jeans in 1920 (and amended by Hermann Bondi, Thomas Gold and Sir Fred

Hoyle in 1948), quickly became a hallmark of scientific independence, asserting that the universe was spatially unbounded, that newly-created matter was perpetually spilling forth from the center of the universe, outspreading, and then filling the void of space. *The idea of a "steady state universe" quickly entered mainstream scientific philosophy, connotating a universe driven and maintained by processes of perpetual creation and evolution.* The notion of *"perpetual creation"* suggested that the universe had no finite beginning, and in that important sense the Steady State Theory was at loggerheads with a Genesis that reported a definite beginning in the words: "Let there be light..." and wherein all of creation had been completed by a deity within six days. Together, the Steady State Theory and Darwinism suggested that the universe not only created and maintained itself, but that it innately contained the forces that led to the creation of life, itself, forces that were entirely random in their modus-operandi. So what need, then, for a divine creator?

That perspective, as it turned out, was a bit premature. In 1927, the Belgian priest-astronomer Georges LeMaitre published a study about the movement of distant galaxies, in which he noted a general *"Doppler Effect,"* or prevailing shift in galactic light toward the *red end* of the visible light spectrum. His findings suggested something entirely new, something that the Steady State Theory couldn't account for—*that the galaxies of the universe might be receding away from some ill-defined centralized point.* Puzzling over this strange finding, LeMaitre suggested that perhaps the universe had been born in *an explosion of some type of primordial atom.* Critics derisively called this the *"Big Bang."* At just about this same point in time, Edwin Hubble stepped forward with conclusive identification of the first stars and galaxies outside of our own galaxy, and *observations which confirmed the fact that all of the observable galaxies were receding at enormous speeds from an apparently common point-of-origin.* In 1939, physicist George Gamow developed *workable scientific hypotheses* around the notion of a "Big Bang," and as a result of his efforts a full-fledged, truly scientific, "Big Bang Theory" emerged into the scientific limelight.

Gamow's work suggested that soon after the great primordial explosion, all space had been filled with high-energy photons, and that these had dispersed, cooled, and evolved into matter. His hypotheses indicated that the universe is a direct product of the forces and matter unleashed by the Big Bang, and these same hypotheses predicted that radiation left over from the Big Bang would ultimately cool into a perpetual, omnipresent, background microwave glow. Discovery of Gamow's so-called "*background radiation*," in 1965, permanently derailed the "Steady State Theory" and proved the fundamental tenets of the "Big Bang Theory"—beyond what many scientists now consider to be reasonable doubt.

General affirmation of the "Big Bang Theory" caused even the most ardent skeptics to admit that the universe had been born at some finite, primordial moment—perhaps in a manner analogous to the description provided in Genesis! For a time, it seemed that science might even come full-circle back to an accommodation of scripture, as in the days of Galileo. Yet, there remained within the scientific community many skeptics of biblical authority, and many advocates of the notion of a randomly-created universe. In a sense, the Steady State Theory had left an indelible mark on science. It was suggested that the Big Bang Universe was nothing more than a result of *a random, accidental explosion*, and that being such it was no more *God-Ordained* than a Steady-State Universe. *The entire issue of scientific-scriptural reconciliation remained open, divisive, and weighted down by history, the errors of the Church, and a mountain of cultural and theological baggage. There was an even thornier problem that precluded scientific affirmation of deity—how could any scientist affirm the existence of a God Who could not be seen, spoken to, or otherwise observed in any way?* No chemist had ever distilled God in a laboratory. No astronomer had ever viewed Him through a telescope. No engineer had ever talked with Him by radio, or telephone. God and His potential relationship to our universe was a scientific mystery, at best! A theology weakened by the Galileo fiasco, evolution, naturalism, and incessant skepticism was simply unable to legitimately address such issues. The only theological safety lay in sticking one's head into the sand and endorsing the sanctity of a literal Bible, even though many theologians knew that the scriptures often contained mistranslation, outright abridgement, and a fundamentally inaccurate view of the real universe. This brings us right up to the present day, and the present problem.

There is still no way to firmly prove the existence of God! The *God Theory* should not be misinterpreted—it only *suggests* that *a strong case* can be made for the existence of The Divine. It also suggests that the view of God which emerges from science is logical and rational, and one which can effectively be used to enhance the power of theology!

CHAPTER ONE

THE PATHS OF ERROR

The universe is the sum total of everything—matter, energy, beings, chemistry, systems, dimensions. Among these, only "beings" are capable of consciously observing the universe and debating its nature. Two separate groups of beings that we know claim intimate comprehension of how the universe works—*"scientists"* and *"theologians."* For ordinary people to follow the lead of either of these groups, however, is very difficult. The two have been moving in very different directions, along different pathways, for nearly four centuries.

Yet, all pathways ultimately have interconnections, and the accumulation of scientific knowledge is rapidly building bridges. As an interdisciplinarian (planner, geographer, geologist), I have gained intimate knowledge of how rapidly interdisciplinary bridges are now being emplaced. Mushrooming scientific knowledge about the universe has provided important new direction in our search for answers to old and hotly-debated issues. The truth remains elusive and enshrouded in an archaic and outdated theology with strong literalistic traditions, traditions devoted to the protection of sacrosanct doctrines and outmoded views of the universe. If theology is to survive, it must be updated, and it must be reshaped to reflect a more realistic view of God and creation.

The *God Theory* is an effort to develop this view. It is a synthesis of theology and science directed at the issue of Who and What God really is. It is not an effort to undo any specific form of theology. It is simply a statement that a new theological view of God and our universe is long overdue. A synthesis of theology and science will be presented in this book to develop that view, demonstrating that the real God *is probably very different, in many ways, yet also very similar, in many ways, to the God of tradition.*

No scientist can dive into theology and come out unscathed. Theology is innately a minefield of unsupported philosophical ideas meshed in tradition and culture—ideas that cannot be tested, scientifically. At the same time, no scientific discipline can exist devoid of philosophy, and all scientific philosophies inevitably enter the mainstream. Scientists have a responsibility to help shape this process of assimilation and effect needed change. My contribution begins with a simple observation that the ancients long ago defined God, and the weight of tradition has imposed their beliefs on us. The Bible, and scripture generally, do not tell us with **precision** Who and What God is. We are told that He is a spirit, that He is the Creator, and that we were created in His Image. But what does this mean? The road to an improved understanding of God begins by spotlighting our own belief systems, and by overturning a few cherished applecarts.

Our present view of deity is rooted in ancient Hebrew monotheism, which is the basis of Christianity, Islam and modern Judaism. Biblical scholars realized long ago that as the tenets of Judaism arose, they were shaped by the dictates of history, culture and politics. The Bible, in other words, has been a continually emerging work of theological leaders (perhaps) based upon their contacts with The Almighty over a very long period of time. It is therefore, innately, the work of mortal and sometimes highly imperfect humans—who may or may not have been divinely inspired—persons who developed and carried notions about the greater scheme of things based upon the available knowledge of the day. Because of this, the final verdict of history is still out on many issues, including the final composition of the Bible. Any detailed study of history, however, makes it crystal clear that the Bible *did not* descend from heaven neatly printed in the King's English, and surrounded by adoring angels.

The first recorded effort to assemble what is now known as the

"Old Testament" was made by *Demetrius of Phaleron*, one of the librarians of the great library of Alexandria, Egypt, around 260 B.C. Termed the "Septuagint," and later the "Alexandrian Canon" it contained 46 books in all, written in the Greek Language. No one knows precisely when these books were translated from the Hebrew into the Greek. However, it is known that during the First Century B.C., Jewish rabbis who remained in Palestine assembled a compilation of 22 holy books, which were later termed the "Palestinian Canon." This version of Old Testament canon was a direct result of the diaspora that followed the Babylonian captivity, an event in which a large number of Jews chose to settle in northern Egypt rather than return to the perilous crossroads that had become the land of Judah. In 383 A.D., Jerome took the 22 books of the Palestinian Canon and merged them with the *additional* 24 books of the Alexandrian Canon that were not in the Palestinian Canon. This represented the first complete assembly of what is now regarded as the Old Testament.

History tells us that the quest to build a Christian holy book probably began with Helena, the mother of the Emperor Constantine, in the 3rd Century A.D. It is known that Helena was a Christian, and that she personally traveled to Jerusalem in an effort to recover artifacts from the time of Jesus. It is possible to speculate that some of her findings may have been presented to attendees of the "Council of Nicaea" in 324 A.D., which formalized the early doctrines and liturgies of the Christian Church. Of course, it was the Nicaean Council (with the support of the Emperor Constantine, who had been converted to Christianity), that considered and adopted the "New Testament" around 350 A.D. Nicea was followed by the Council of Hippo in 393 A.D., and the Council of Carthage in 397 A.D., both in North Africa. The most important outputs of these assemblies were a New Testament consisting of 27 books, and an Old Testament consisting of Jerome's revised Canon. There were in those days important differences about what should and should not be included in the Bible. Coptic Christians came up with a radically different and unique version of the New Testament including the supposedly secret words of Jesus. The Christian Church of Syria, on the other hand, refused to accept the Book of Revelation. The Roman Catholic Church accepts the work of Nicaea, Hippo and Carthage, but did not officially ratify its own version of the Bible until the "Council of Trent" in 1546. At Trent, the Alexandrian Canon was adopted, and hundreds of letters were reviewed, along with dozens of books and gospels purported to have been written by the apostles, or by early Christian leaders and scholars. The result was ratification of 27 *"divinely-inspired" books, as per the Council of Carthage, and the addition of seven "apocryphal" books which were recognized as "non-inspired," but of significant historical importance.* The Apocrypha expanded the Roman Catholic Bible to a total of 73 books, versus the 66 which came out of the three early councils and now constitute the protestant Bible.

It is clear that the Roman Catholic clergy at Trent used official standards, or "canon," as the basis for determining whether a document should be included in the New Testament. Earlier councils did the same, but being less distant temporally from the life and ministry of Jesus, there seems to have been more of a feel for what Jesus actually taught. In all of the early councils, there was much debate about what should and should not be included. Scores of gospels and epistles were considered for inclusion in the Bible and rejected. In no case did God come down and make the final decision. Men assembled the Bible, not God. Moreover, during (and after) the decision-making process there was disagreement on the issue of divine inspiration and leadership, and what should and should not be included in the holy book. This same plight continues to this very day. Today, for example, the Christian Church in Syria continues to disavow the Book of Revelation, and there are increasingly powerful theologians in America and Western Europe who believe that the "Gospel of Thomas," which was found in Egypt in 1945, should be added to the New Testament. Even evangelical and fundamentalist scholars recognize that omissions, mistranslations and unwarranted additions have been made to scripture, and many of these are actively being corrected. Retrospectively, however, it remains clear that the

New Testament was assembled at a time when historians kept detailed records, and it is therefore known with some precision how the New Testament came into being. The same cannot be said of either the Alexandrian or Palestinian Canon, i.e. the basis for the Old Testament.

The 46 books of the Old Testament are, indeed, old. They also differ markedly in origin and purpose from that of the New Testament books. Rather than being concerned with the life of a single person, as in the New Testament, the Old Testament is derived from the Alexandrian and Palestinian canon, and functions as a mythic chronicle and detailed history of the State of Israel and its relationship to the Almighty. Portions of it may have been assembled as far back as the 10th Century B.C. Other portions of it did not appear until the 2nd or perhaps even the 1st Century B.C. Given the enormous timeframe over which it was assembled, much information about individual authors of Old Testament books has now been unavoidably lost. Tradition has it that Moses authored portions of the first five books of the Old Testament, and biblical scholars recognize a very close temporal connection to Moses in the "Yahwist" genre, which is distinct and highly recognizable, prosaically, and theologically. A critical point for Christians is that the books of the Old Testament were not considered sacred *and inviolable* (in the strict Christian tradition) until long after their composition. Their composition *and revision* clearly occurred and sometimes spanned decades, or even centuries. As new theological views emerged, old and outmoded ideas occasionally became fair game for editing and/or abridgement. The book of Genesis clearly contains evidence of opposing visions of the Hebrew state and its religious ideals, as well as substantial evidence of editing that reflects the evolution of Jewish theology in concert with fundamental socio-cultural concerns which are still being debated in Jewish society, today.

John Shelby Spong, in *Rescuing the Bible from Fundamentalism*, notes that much of the Old Testament can be traced to *four differing rabbinical genre*, each with a differing vision of the Jewish Nation and its relationship to deity. These genre are also recognized by the vast majority of biblical scholars, and they are actively studied at virtually every major seminary. *Understanding these genre and their respective goals and contributions is a must in order to properly interpret Old Testament scriptures.*

The oldest, or *"Yahwist,"* genre was closest to Moses, and packaged the original written, scriptural history of the Jewish nation, including an account of creation beginning with Verse 4 of Chapter 2, a description of immediate post-creational events in Chapters 2, 3 and 4, and original descriptions of The Almighty and His Divine Revelation. It is relatively certain that the Yahwists arrived upon the scene around 960 B.C., and that they recorded the original, oral accounts of Adam and Eve, Abraham, Isaac, Jacob and Joseph. They also chronicled the Hebrew exodus from Egypt and the subsequent establishment of a temple and monarchy at Jerusalem. Some of the Yahwist ideals were soon disputed by a second distinct genre called the *"Elohists,"* who arrived upon the scene around 850 B.C. The Elohists lived in Samaria, and were driven by a desire to justify separation of the Jewish Northern Kingdom, Israel, from the southern kingdom of Judah. *Elohist scriptures thus reduce the importance of Jerusalem to Jewish worship*—largely by emphasizing the important religious shrines of the northern kingdom, such as Beersheba and Bethel, and by tying these to great national patriarchs such as Abraham, Isaac, and Jacob. The Elohists clearly disagreed with the fundamental Yahwist thesis that God's covenant had been made only with Moses and his successors, and they edited the sacred story to assert that God's covenant had been directly made with the people on Mt. Horeb, in a profound event which allowed them to interact directly with God.

The *Deuteronomists*, who surfaced after the Elohists, represent a third major genre to profoundly shape the Old Testament, and their work was largely devoted to undoing much of the Elohist influence. They arrived upon the scene soon after the Assyrians had conquered the Northern Kingdom of Israel and carried 10 of the 12 Hebrew tribes away into captivity. In the shadow of this horrible event, the Deuteronomists edited the scriptures to construct a coherent theological rationale for what had happened, one which would hopefully help the remaining Hebrew Tribes to avoid such a fate in the future. Their efforts directly attributed this great tragedy to the failure of the Israelites to obey the *letter of the law*. And to correct this problem, they instilled many meticulous new laws and reforms aimed at cleansing the people in the sight of God.

Despite rabbinical efforts to spare Judah the fate of the northern kingdom, Jerusalem fell to the Babylonians in 596 B.C., resulting in the enslavement of the two remaining tribes of Israel in the exotic land of the Chaldeans (Babylonians). This event, which is extremely well-documented historically and scripturally, precipitated the rise of a fourth genre, the *"Priestly Perspective,"* which represents a de facto theocratic leadership that held the nation together during the Babylonian experience. The Hebrew priests of Babylon formed the glue that ultimately cemented and preserved the Hebrew nation through extremely great adversity, *and this is a tremendously important point.* Like the earlier Deuteronomists, these rabbis believed that the destruction of the Jewish Nation had occurred because of the failure of the people to obey the "letter of the Law." They believed that this failure had inevitably provoked the ire of a wrathful God. Under this conviction, they thoroughly edited the scriptures to include stringent new laws and worship standards, and to show that God could be extremely wrathful in the face of disobedience. They believed that all of this was necessary to impress upon the people the need for strict obedience to God's Laws. Under their influence, much (perhaps most) of the biblical books of Exodus, Leviticus and Numbers came into being. They also "thoroughly edited" (Spong, 1991, p.53) earlier versions of the sacred story, including the First Chapter of Genesis and the Ten Commandments. Some of their major contributions include shoring-up waning traditions such as circumcision and observance of the Sabbath. At the same time, the biblical book of Daniel shows that many Jewish leaders were educated by the Babylonians, in an effort to instill in them the "arts of the Chaldeans." Not surprisingly, then, the scriptures necessarily came to reflect important Babylonian influences, including Mesopotamian mythology. As the Old Testament was being revised, such external influences were also doubtlessly being "revised in."

In summation, it should be emphasized that *the original Old Testament scriptures were assembled from the distinct and often diametrically antithetical writings of the* Yahwists and Elohists. Both of these contributions were then edited, altered and abridged—first by the Deuteronomists, and later by those of the "Priestly Perspective" in Babylon. Without a doubt, editing and abridgement has also been conducted by other genre and individuals who cannot now be identified.

It is my belief that a great portion of the discrepancies between ancient Hebrew scripture and science can be traced to Babylon, and to the revisory work of the Priestly Perspective. Today, there are essentially two ways that we can view Old Testament editing: (1) either the original Divine Revelation issued by God and recorded by the Yahwists was incomplete and required much further "Divine Elaboration," or (2) the scriptures were changed merely to reflect changing Hebrew cultural, political and religious views. Obviously, horrific events such as the fall of Jerusalem and the enslavement of the people in Babylon had a major effect upon the emerging theology and written scriptures, and as reinterpretation occurred the scriptures were often changed to reflect the newly emerging views, as well as the host of biblical characters and events that continued to emerge.

Prose, parallelism, flow and writing style indicate that Genesis 1:1-3, in addition to Genesis 2:4-26, comprised the original, Yahwist Creation Story. In the view of the Graf-Wellhausen school of biblical scholars (Spong, 1991) most of Chapters 2 through 4 of Genesis definitely belong to the Yahwist genre, and were thus written between 960 and 920 B.C. Similarly, prosaic patterns, styles and message assign Genesis 1:4-31 and 2:1-3 to the Priestly Perspective (of Babylon). This is a very important point, because it means that all but the first three verses of the creation story of the First Chapter of Genesis were added *after* 596 B.C. How much, if any, of this passage was provided earlier, then revised by the priests of Babylon, will always be at question. If this creation story existed in the original

Yahwist or Elohist text, it was certainly completely rewritten in the prose of the Hebrew priests of Babylon, and it is probable that they made major alterations. The presentation of passages written in 596 B.C. *before* the original Yahwist account of creation (which was written about 400 years earlier, in roughly 960 B.C., and which now appears in the *Second Chapter* of Genesis) significantly changes the tone of the original sacred creation story (Spong, 1991, p. 43-55).[3]

One of the most obvious differences between parts of Chapter One (evidencing the "Priestly Perspective"), and Chapter Two (evidencing the original "Yahwist" genre), is the application of time. *The Yahwist creation story makes **no mention of time**,* except in a very general sense (e.g. "*...in the DAY that the Lord God made the earth and the heavens...*"). **It is clear that the Yahwists used the term "day" exclusively in reference to generalized *spheres of time*.** They did not divide the events of creation into discrete 24-hour "days," nor did they create six 24-hour-day creation cycles. The six-day creation cycle is exclusively a product of editing by a priestly genre that came along 400 years after the Divine Revelation of God to Moses. It was necessary for the Hebrew priests of Babylon to add distinct timeframes showing that God created the universe in six days, in order for them to show that God rested on the Sabbath, as an example for the Jewish people to follow:

> Under pressure from these priestly writers, the familiar seven-day creation story that opens our Bibles was written to root Sabbath day observance in the moment of creation. The God who rested from creation on the Sabbath hallowed this day and mandated its observance by all those who would be the people of this God. This account of creation was in fact one of the last parts of the Hebrew Scriptures to be written... (Spong, 1991, p.53)[4]

The need to observe the "Sabbath" created problems. Six other days had to be conjured and integrated into the creation story before a seventh day could and its required religious observance could even be discussed. So, the creation story was edited to show that everything was completed in six distinct stages prior to the Sabbath, and that God had justified the Sabbath as a day of rest from the labors of creation, by His example.

To the Hebrew priests of Babylon, the editing of the creation story was not a theological correction or convenience, but a matter of normal theological evolution and national survival! A diaspora had been initiated. Many of the Jews who had not been carried away into Babylon had fled Israel for the safety of Egypt, and many of those who had been taken captive in Babylon were actively abandoning their heritage and were being absorbed into the majority population. Ensuring the assembly of the people in synagogues on the Sabbath was just about the only way to guarantee that they would absorb unadulterated Hebrew religious and cultural values. Without such drastic means, most of the Jewish population might have been totally assimilated into the much larger Babylonian majority.

So, in a very real sense, the terms "day," "evening," and "morning" are only markers of the priestly effort to save and preserve the Jewish nation. A literalistic interpretation of the First Chapter of Genesis cannot possibly show what was going on behind the scenes, and cannot possibly capture the real meaning of the scriptures. For a 21st Century Christian gentile (or Jew) to interpret the First Chapter of Genesis without reference to these events is the height of fallacy.

The great Indian leader Mahatma Ghandi contributed some important ideas about religion that can help us place these problems in their proper perspective. Ghandi believed that all religions were given to us by God, but that all suffer from a common problem called **"double distillation."** According to this precept, all major religions came to us originally as a product of divine revelation, but the scriptures that later form the basis for religious observance (of that revelation) inevitably become a victim of changing human needs, values, cultures and popular ideals. Ghandi believed that God had regularly delivered authentic "Divine Truths" into human hands, but that human instability had just as routinely found ways of substituting error for truth.

And whom should we blame for this? Should we blame the Jews for wanting to survive, the Babylonians for invading Palestine and threatening the survival of Judah, the Persians for conquering Babylon and releasing the Jews who carried their abridged version of scripture to Egypt, the Greeks who staffed the Library of Alexandria and received the Septuagint, or the Egyptians for the original Hebrew captivity and the creation of a perpetual national insecurity? While we're at it, perhaps we should blame Donald Duck, and his nephews Huey, Dewey and Louie! In truth, blame is irrelevant, and fact is all that is of importance. It has been known for centuries that Genesis was a collage of editings and revisions, but the fact of the matter is that one doesn't sell religion to a world that knows nothing about God and Jewish history by promoting a view that the Hebrew scriptures are inaccurate. The blame therefore falls squarely upon the theological leaders who have ignored the truth, perpetuated fallacy in the name of expediency, and failed to correct problems that have been obvious for quite a bit longer than a coon's age.

Genesis, in summation, is plagued by two major problems that impede absorption of the Bible's creation story into a scientifically enlightened 21st Century world. The first problem has to do with the Ptolemaic model of the universe that is inherently encapsulated within its language and tone (see the introductory chapter). The second problem has to do with the six-day creation cycle. Both problems were created during the Babylonian captivity. Neither existed when the original Divine Revelation was issued by God to Moses. While a strong case can be made for treating creation days as loose "spheres of time" rather than discrete 24-hour days, as I will show in Chapter Nine, the fact that human beings are the probable instigators and conjurers of the "creation-day concept" means that only human beings should be blamed for the error brought to the table, and this blame needs to be cited either in: (1) biblical footnotes, or (2) through an expansion of biblical text to better reflect time, place and circumstance. When the Bible was being assembled, many scriptures, epistles and books were culled and eliminated because they did not meet the standards (canon) recognized by those who attended the Council of Nicea. Eliminating inappropriate language and passages from existing scriptures would only serve the same purpose that was pursued at Nicaea, Hippo, Carthage and Trent—the perfection of the Word.

In general, unacceptable barriers between modern science and theology are rooted in the Babylonian captivity. While Babylon gave us great heroes like Daniel, it also provided the legacy of an altered creation story, an inaccurate model of the universe, and significant changes in the Jewish Law. There is also significant evidence that some of the Babylonian arts, sciences, traditions and folklore infiltrated into Hebrew culture during the captivity, and that they ultimately made their way into the Hebrew scriptures—specifically making stories such as Noah's Ark and the Tower of Babel highly suspect.

There is a major difference between "Divine Revelation" and a story told by ancient men (and/or women) to illustrate the power and perhaps the "Divine Will" of God. Parables are used throughout the Bible to elucidate how God deals with us and our world. The problem with literalism is that it doesn't allow us to distinguish between what is Divine Revelation and what is Divine Parable. It rams the entire Bible with all of its paradox, innuendoes, editings and oddities down our collective throats as "Divine Revelation." By ignoring the need to reconcile scripture and science, theologians have slowly and unwittingly undermined the notion of a perfect God, Who (according to scripture) is inherently incapable of lying. The proper course is one in which real Divine Revelation squares with ***proven knowledge*** about our universe. All theologians must recognize a simple fact—that God would not create a universe and then give us an account of His creation process that was untrue. Thus, "reality" and "revelation" are linked. In the final analysis, real or true "Divine Revelation" is inherently impossible to refute by scientific or other valid means. Any theology that holds otherwise is, at best, half-baked.

Conversely, anything that can be refuted by science, artifacts or whatever, cannot be "Divine Revelation," and is either the result of human "double-distillation" or simply a parable that was never intended for sacrosanct status. A major first step in coming to an understanding of God is simply to shake the bugs out of our literalistic theology—bugs that have nestled themselves in archaic ignorance, bad science and superstition. This is not to say that theology is replete with bugs, it is to say that *a few* significant blunders have been wrapped into tradition and passed on without due consideration. The reality of the situation is that scripture is an inherent compendium of history, politics, cultural norms, and *occasionally* even the actual, Divine Word of The Almighty. Much of the Old Testament can therefore only be taken at face value, in the sense that it reflects a decidedly *Hebrew* face.

CHAPTER TWO

FOUNDATIONS OF THE UNIVERSE

The search for God is as old as human intelligence. Some of the early Greeks believed that a giant named Atlas stood atop a giant tortoise and held up the world. The American Indians believed in a mystical spirit who sometimes appeared in the form of a white buffalo and controlled every aspect of nature. The natives of Fiji believed that a God named "Rokomautu" scooped sand and mud from the bottom of the ocean, in great handfuls, and created dry land. The Athenians viewed their gods as powerful, yet capricious beings who were fond of tinkering with the world from a detached observatory atop Mt. Olympus. The Jews gave us the notion of a single omnipotent God and a thrilling account of how He created a universe steeped in a rich framework of physical order and Divine Harmony.

How do we find God—and if, per chance, we should find Him, how can we ever hope to understand Him? The great 16th Century protestant theologian, John Calvin, argued against attempting to rationalize God, and contended that all we need to know about The Almighty is contained within the scriptures. Calvin believed that scripture is a gift from God for everyone, designed to lead us into a personal relationship with The Creator. He contended that the scriptures dealt primarily with the appearance of things and avoided scientific precision—in order to permit simple and uneducated individuals to find their own way to God. According to Calvin's rationale, scientific knowledge opened individuals to a deeper understanding of the scriptures, but there was no real need to integrate science and scripture, because what God really wanted from us was *us*. Calvin therefore elevated personal scriptural study and individual communion with God to a very high status. Calvinist ideals helped spread Christianity because they told Christians that God had come down to their level, that the realities of a complex physical world could be safely ignored as long as individuals cultivated a meaningful *personal* relationship with their Creator. Calvinism cemented the notion among fundamentalists that *science and scripture really do not need to be reconciled,* that what really counts is moral and spiritual reconciliation, and continuing communion with God.

The primary problem with Calvinism is that John Calvin lived 500 years ago. Today, the world is complex, dynamic and challenging, and some knowledge of science is essential. Yet, serious study of science inevitably leads to questions about the origin and authority of the scriptures. Recognizing this, catholic and mainstream protestant denominations have tried to gain improved understanding of the ties between science and theology. In 1951, the Vatican formed a special council which studied the Big Bang Theory and eventually found it to be "harmonious" with biblical teachings. In 1997, under the leadership of Pope John Paul II, another Vatican council at least partially embraced *evolution.*

Such efforts are far from unique. Lutherans and Anglicans embraced science and naturalism during the 18th Century, and have generally held their ground. Anglicans assimilated the notion of "Natural Theology" during the 19th Century, and began to see their church as the "mother of knowledge," and the Bible and its creation story as the supreme manifestation of science. According to this theme, everything unfolded from God's design, including science, itself, and science could not, therefore, help but to demonstrate the omnipotence of God and the marvelous order and rationale of Creation[5]:

> Natural philosophers surveyed their labors with a notably devotional atmosphere. Boyle and Newton, for example, did not make the sharp modern distinction between science and theology, and they were highly serious about both their theological and their scientific

studies.[6]

But in the 19th Century, the doctrine of natural theology hit a snag called "Darwinism." Darwinism and other outputs of the "Age of Rationalism" drove wedges into the ties between scientists and theologians, and caused "natural theology" to fall from favor. The rise of atheism on the heels of Darwinism only cemented the barriers. According to Peacocke, the founding of the natural sciences played a fundamental role in this schism:

> The development of geology as a science, with the discovery of the character of the Earth's processes, had an effect on man's view of himself and his own history. This was dramatically compounded when, after Darwin, man found himself a natural part of the history of organic life... Thus, there was a genuine new theological question which had to be posed in response to a shift in the understanding of the natural world.[7]

Before Darwin and Hutton, man was viewed as a separate and special creation, and the Earth was thought to be only a few thousand years old. Most landforms were thought to have originated in Noah's Flood. The rise of the natural sciences changed all of these notions, but not without intense controversy:

> Then, as now, the participants were basically divided into, on the one hand, the 'reconcilers', who thought Darwinism and evolution compatible with Christian belief; and, on the other hand, the 'irreconcilers', who thought them incompatible, either on behalf of an infallible religion or an all-embracing science. On the whole, the *irreconcilers* of both kinds, that is, both pro- and anti-Christian, made the most noise and so created the situation that we still, by and large, inherit—of the Christian religion and natural science retreating to their

respective territories, leaving a no-man's land between, enshrouded in the numbing silence of an uneasy truce.[8]

This is an important observation, because it suggests that most Christians have been forced into a rejection of the natural sciences by their loudmouthed brethren. This is not a tenable 21st Century position. Before the new millennium has passed, our descendants will have traversed the solar system and neighboring stars. Out in the awesome and majestic pinwheel arms of the Milky Way, the greatest reality will be the incomprehensible vastness of space, its billions of brilliant suns, its vibrant solar systems, its beautiful galaxies. Those living among the stars will be forced to adopt new realities that an ancient, literalistic theology will not be able to accommodate. Just as Copernicanism triumphed over Ptolemaic notions of the universe and the Dark Ages gave way to an era of enlightenment, so literalism will give way to a rational new theology.

This "new rationalism" is already upon us. It is in large part a result of longstanding scientific trends in which atheism has been discredited. More than anything else, however, it stems from the validation of the "Big Bang Theory," and a recognition among many scientists that the Big Bang Theory substantiates the notion of a *Divine Creation*. The distinguished astronomer Robert Jastrow poignantly drives this point home in his book *God and the Astronomers*:

> When an astronomer writes about God, his colleagues assume he is either over the hill or going bonkers. In my case it should be understood from the start that I am an agnostic in religious matters. However, I am fascinated by some strange developments going on in astronomy—partly because of their religious implications and partly because of the peculiar reactions of my colleagues.
>
> The essence of the strange developments is that the Universe had, in some sense, a beginning—that it began

at a certain moment in time, and under circumstances that seem to make it impossible—not just now, but EVER—to find out what force or forces brought the world into being at that moment.[9]

Jastrow goes on to describe how the scientific community was initially hostile toward the Big Bang Theory, reveling in the "*freedom from theology*" provided by the Steady State Theory. Thus, it was difficult for many scientists to make the rational and psychological shift. Most had trouble with the Big Bang Theory's fundamental assertion that the universe came into being as a result of a single, dramatic event. The notion of a *finite creation event* smacked far too strongly of the First Chapter of Genesis. To others, it simply "smacked" and "bounced," as evidenced in this excerpt of physicist A.S. Eddington:

> Philosophically, the notion of an abrupt beginning to the present order of Nature is repugnant to me, as I think it must be to most; and even those who would welcome a proof of the intervention of a Creator will probably consider that a single windingup at some remote epoch is not really the kind of relation between God and his world that brings satisfaction to the mind.[10]

Yet, the Big Bang Theory has become a steamroller, smashing all opposition, and spelling a brave new relationship between scientists and liberal-to-moderate theologians. *The God Theory* is only one in a long line of books and publications reflecting this new synthesis. However, the basis of *The God Theory* was long ago developed in Feynmann's definition of truth, in the doctrine of natural theology, and in the words of Deuteronomy and Psalms. Moreover, "Divine Revelation" is *always* consistent with reality; whereas the "nondivine" can be identified by its perpetual non-reality—its opposition to *proven* scientific knowledge. An associated idea, of course, is that God exists. The great quest of the *God Theory*, on the other hand, is to determine who and what God really is. To allow us to focus on the essential *basis* and *quest* of the *God Theory*, two hypotheses have been formulated: (1) that the universe is integral to The Creator and His creative activities, and (2) The Creator is an integral product of the most fundamental realm of the universe.

The organization of the remainder of this book is predicated on these two hypotheses. In suggesting that the universe is integral to the Creator (Hypothesis #1), we are rejecting the Ptolemaic model of a God Who is apart and aloof from nature, and in saying that the universe is integral to God's creative activities we are placing Him right in the middle of what is happening. In saying that God is, Himself, a product of our universe (Hypothesis #2) we are saying that an explanation of God lies in science—in natural phenomena associated with our universe that can be rationalized and explained. Chapters Seven and Eight will deal intensively with this hypothesis. Just in case you haven't noticed, both hypotheses reflect and, indeed, are integral to the ongoing synthesis of science and scripture.

The basis of this synthesis, as noted heretofore, is the "Big Bang Theory," and it is therefore appropriate that we begin our quest for God with a sketch and overview of that theory.

The Big Bang is regarded by many scientists as *a proven fact, sustained in an accidental discovery, in 1964, by astronomers Arno Penzias and Robert Wilson* (who at the time were working at the Bell Laboratories in New Jersey). As these two unwitting pioneers actively scanned the heavens with a new microwave detector something very important happened:

> Penzias and Wilson were worried when they found that their detector was picking up more noise than it ought to. The noise did not appear to be coming from any particular direction. First they discovered bird droppings in their detector and checked for other possible malfunctions, but soon ruled these out. They knew that any noise from within the atmosphere would

be stronger when the detector was not pointing straight up than when it was, because light rays travel through much more atmosphere when received from near the horizon than when received from directly overhead. The extra noise was the same whichever direction the detector was pointed, so it must come from outside the atmosphere. It was also the same day and night and throughout the year, even though the earth was rotating on its axis and orbiting around the sun. This showed that the radiation must come from beyond the Solar System, and even from beyond the galaxy, as otherwise it would vary as the movement of Earth pointed the detector in different directions. In fact, we know that the radiation must have traveled to us across most of the observable universe, and since it appears to be the same in different directions, the universe must also be the same in every direction, if only on a large scale. We now know that whichever direction we look, this noise never varies by more than one part in ten thousand—so Penzias and Wilson had unwittingly stumbled across a remarkably accurate confirmation of Friedmann's first assumption *(that the universe is identical in whichever direction we look)*.

At roughly the same time two American physicists at nearby Princeton University, Bob Dicke and Jim Peebles, were also taking an interest in microwaves. They were working on a suggestion, made by George Gamow (once a student of Alexander Friedmann), that the early universe should have been very hot and dense, glowing white-hot. Dicke and Peebles argued that we should still be able to see the glow of the early universe, because light from very distant parts of it would only just be reaching us now. However, the expansion of the universe meant that this light should be so greatly red-shifted that it would appear to us now as microwave radiation. Dicke and Peebles were preparing to look for this radiation when Penzias and Wilson heard about their work and realized that they had already found it. For this, Penzias and Wilson were awarded the Nobel Prize in 1978.[11] (Note: italicized remarks are mine.)

The importance of this discovery remained controversial for the following 27 years. Then in 1992, COBE (Cosmic Research Background Explorer) satellite observations discovered minute fluctuations in the microwave glow, precisely as predicted by laws of quantum physics. It was precisely the pattern of fluctuation that had been expected. In 1997, astrophysicist George Smoot of the Lawrence Berkeley Laboratory announced the discovery of massive wisps of gas, as much as ten billion light years across, far larger than any of the galaxies or galaxy clusters contained within our universe. These unbelievably massive clouds are now seen as overt visible relics of the Big Bang. They are clouds of gas which never condensed enough to form galaxies, but their presence confirms Gamow's assertion that matter condensed from the fires of the Big Bang—first into gases, then into dense gases, and finally into galaxies.

Indeed, the Big Bang can be likened to the creative *Hand of God*—a hand that ***introduced matter into the universe and released the forces of nature in a way that gave the universe form—and not just any old form but a very specific and unique form that favored the development of ever-more- complex natural systems. In this complexity lies our being.*** The Big Bang was therefore a special event. To understand it, we need to take another close look at the words of Jastrow:

> Because of complications introduced by the branch of physics called quantum mechanics, their (physicists) predictions do not start in the very instant of the explosion at which time the density was infinite—but only 10^{-43} seconds after that moment, when the density was finite, but a staggering 10^{90} tons per cubic inch. AT

THIS STAGE ALL OF THE UNIVERSE THAT WE CAN SEE TODAY WAS PACKED INTO THE SPACE OF AN ATOMIC NUCLEUS. The pressure and temperature were also extremely high, and the Universe was a fiery sea of radiation, from which particles emerged only to fall back, disappearing and reappearing ceaselessly.[12]

At first, pure energy was manifested in a giant ball of light, and a vast sea of energy spilled forth in quantum bursts from whatever exploded. These bursts of energy were indelibly recorded in the temperature fluctuations of the microwave glow discovered by Wilson and Penzias, a glow which remains available for our inspection and analysis even today. Then, subatomic particles emerged along the cutting edge of creation, and gravity made its appearance. The almost unfathomable temperatures within the fireball initially and briefly caused gravity to become repulsive instead of attractive, and matter was hurled outward at enormous speed. Augmented by this wild, super-repulsive protogravity, the stuff of creation was strewn across the void of space at speeds far greater than the speed of light. In an astonishingly short time the universe inflated into a massive entity. After inflation ebbed, heat and radiation had been spread relatively thin, and space began to cool. Gravity then became an "attractive" force, and proceeded to give the universe form and substance. Sub-atomic particles condensed from the heat of the explosion were segregated into electrons, protons and neutrons, and then hydrogen atoms. Pockets of hydrogen then segregated into hydrogen isotopes and helium. By this process, space became lumpy, gasclouds formed and condensed into proto-galaxies. Over the next few billions of years, stars formed, evolved, and exploded, and in this process churned out heavier and heavier elements into the evolving universe, gradually building the material basis of our existing universe and the complex molecular basis of life.

The importance of gravity in the formation of our universe cannot be overemphasized. Its importance is nearly equal to that of the explosion, itself. Gravity successively turned subatomic particles into atoms, gasclouds, galaxies, suns, new elements, new suns, new elements, and ultimately our own solar system. It then caused the accretion of our planet, solidified its crust and formed its tectonic plates. It then kept those plates in motion, and thereby gradually transformed the Earth's surface into a suitable place for life. Once life appeared, it provided for the organization of microtubules in the cytoskeleton of developing cells, without which there could not be the form and pattern essential to truly complex lifeforms. Indeed, as will become clear in the final chapters of this book, without gravity the universe would not exist.

As the physical universe took shape, gravity gave it form, order, and vitality, and set the forces of evolution in motion. As life emerged, gravity gave it form, order, and vitality, and further set the forces of evolution in motion. Without gravity, there would be no universe, no galaxies, no solar systems, no planets, no Earth, no atmosphere, no oceans, no soils, no plants, no animals, *and no us.* In a very, very important sense, then, gravity corresponds to the creative Hand of God in motion. It ties us intimately to the Big Bang, and (as we shall see in subsequent chapters) to events that occurred *before* the Big Bang, and which can be elucidated by a composite of science and scripture. Perhaps it also ties us to The Almighty; and to events on the other side of eternity that have heretofore been beyond our comprehension.

Einstein's "Theory of General Relativity" suggests that the universe began with a big bang and that it will die in a "big crunch." According to Hawking:

> Einstein's general theory of relativity, on its own, predicted that space-time began at the big bang singularity and would come to an end either at the big crunch singularity (if the whole universe recollapsed), or at a singularity inside a black hole...[13]

The notion of a "big crunch" stems from a recognition of the destructive power of gravity. Gravity is thus a creator *and* a destroyer. It straddles the doorstep of eternity and simultaneously plays up to both sides. The notion of a "Big Crunch" is not just any old idea; it is an idea developed by perhaps the most brilliant human mind that ever existed—that of Einstein. It tells of a process larger than our universe, larger even than time—something called "eternity." We know that the universe was created by an explosion and shaped by gravity, and the Big Crunch tells that in the end gravity will destroy the universe it initially formed. So it is that gravity becomes the primary driving force behind the great caissons of eternity.

Borrowing from the Greek, we can identify *two primary phases of matter in the universe*, the ***alpha*** and the ***omega*** *phases*—"alpha" denoting *created-phase* matter, and "omega" denoting the *destroyed-phase*. Thus, we can say that matter is inherently dichotomous, that as the universe enters an alpha phase, it automatically evolves toward the omega phase, and vice-versa. We can also think of these phases in terms of the ***relative*** activities of *energy* and *matter*. During the initial explosive subphase of the alpha cycle, the universe is heavily dominated by energy, but gradually thereafter the ratio of energy to matter decreases. Then, at some point in time the universe collapses into a colossal black hole, and following gravitational collapse, it is dominated by matter. In this omega phase, the universe becomes little more than a **formless mass**. Suddenly, the trail of science leads to the doorstep of Genesis 1:2, and our first composite of science and scripture—a composite telling us something about *what might have existed before the Big Bang*:

> And the earth was *without form and void*; and *darkness was upon the face of the deep*...[14]

The phrase "without form and void" has obvious application in descriptions of black holes. Such objects can be considered *FORM*less because light cannot escape them, they can be considered *VOID*less because the substance of which they are composed is gravitationally crushed to near-infinite density, leaving no remaining void space between sub-atomic particles. Can it be that Genesis supplements the Big Bang Theory to suggest that our universe was in the form of a black hole prior to the Big Bang? Here we have the entire universe encased in a black hole prior to creation, and our own Earth an implicit part of this omega-phase universe, so that the language of Genesis applyies equally to the Earth and the universe. The two are one and integral and "without form and void" in the *exact* phraseology that appears in Genesis 1:2. All of a sudden, the scriptures seem to contain great hidden truths unimaginable to biblical literalists.

The notion of a Big Crunch is not just a ponderous hypothetical exercise, it is an active process that we can see unfolding in our universe, even today. In 1995, a black hole was identified in our galaxy at about 100 million light years from the Earth. This object was estimated to be the size of an average "thumbnail," yet its impact on surrounding objects indicated a mass of roughly *1.2 billion suns! So gravitationally potent was it that it had swallowed up all of the surrounding matter within a circumference of roughly 5 light years.* The destructive power of such objects is awesome! Their potential role in reshaping the universe can only be grasped when we realize that in a universe of 500 billion galaxies, there may be as many as two or three trillion black holes.

Astronomers have determined that black holes are continually forming, and the prevailing evidence suggests that as these objects come on line, a corresponding portion of the material "alpha-phase" universe goes off line. With each passing day, the universe is taking on proportionately more of the gravitationally-enhanced "omega-phase matter"—the stuff dubbed "dark matter" by astronomers. At some point in transition between the alpha and the omega, it only stands to reason that black holes will gain preponderant power over the remaining alpha-phase universe. Evidence of this burgeoning "black hole control" is already implicit in a *hierarchy of black holes that has been observed and confirmed to exist in all quarters of the observable universe*. Astronomical studies have shown a vast size-range for black holes, from those that are "supermassive," controlling great clusters of galaxies across millions of light years, to those which are relatively tiny, controlling only a few objects within a few light weeks or months. The fact that a hierarchy of black holes exists is of overwhelming importance because it provides physical evidence of a progressive aggregation of *dark matter*. An infinite continuation of such an aggregative process is most likely to end in a Big Crunch.

This progressive aggregation of dark matter is natural because black holes form naturally as stars begin to exhaust their fuel and die. Any aging star, at some point in time, will begin to exhaust its nuclear fuel, and as this occurs it is inevitably driven into recurring phases of expansion and/or contraction in hopeless attempts to balance the available fuel against ongoing internal reactions. In the final phases of its existence several alternatives are possible—a dying star can collapse to a small, rocky mass and remain in that state forever, or it can gradually shrink in size and brilliance in hundreds of phases of expansion and collapse, or it may explode suddenly and cataclysmically—dying the picturesque death of a supernova. No two stars ever die in precisely the same manner. The larger a star is, the hotter it will burn, the quicker it will die, and the more likely it is to become a black hole during its death throes.

In 1928, an Indian graduate student named Subrahmanyan Chandrasekhar found that when the "cold mass" of a star is more than roughly 1.5 times the mass of our sun, gravity will overcome repulsive forces operative in the star's interior, and the star will suddenly collapse to infinite density! It may instantaneously become a "thumbnail-sized" black hole in space, whereupon its focused mass engenders an instantaneous mushrooming of gravitational energy. Depending upon its initial size and the density of matter in surrounding space, such an object may be able to grow and gain gravitational control over a large region of the universe, as we have seen.

More black holes would form were it not for the fact that stars are naturally resistant to collapse. As a star begins to collapse, gravitational compression greatly accelerates internal sub-atomic movement, and this brings into play something called "Pauli

Exclusion Principle Repulsion." The "Pauli Exclusion Principle" is a basic law of physics which provides that no two real particles (particles of matter) can occupy the same exact position in space. Pauli Principle repulsion means that as a star is gravitationally compressed, and as its subatomic particles come into increasing proximity to each other, increasing levels of electromagnetic repulsion are generated which speed up particle movement to avoid collision. Thus, a collapsing star automatically generates powerful counter-forces that tend to stop collapse, and which may even promote expansion after a round of collapse.

A star's ultimate fate, however, is determined by the overall balance of compressive and repulsive forces. Natural Pauli Principle repulsion normally averts complete collapse. However, there are limits to everything. Einstein's Special Theory of Relativity, expressed in the formula $E=MC^2$, provides that the speed of light is the maximum attainable velocity of any object or particle. In effect, once the mass of a collapsing stellar object has forced internal atomic movement to the speed of light, no further acceleration of internal particles can be achieved, and at that point the star has no further resistance to gravitational compression. Toss in a straw and the so-called "Chandrasekhar Limit" will be exceeded! The result will be an instantaneous collapse, and this collapse will immediately give birth to a gravitational field so strong that not even light can escape it—a "black hole" will come into being in every sense of the word. Any black hole is inherently "without void" because its internal matter has been packed so densely by gravitational collapse that no inter-particle space remains. A black hole is simultaneously "formless" because it cannot be seen, and because its density and gravitational power is so great that not even light can escape it. The surrounding portion of space is pervasively affected by all of this, and the environment necessarily becomes a literal manifestation of the Genesis phrase: "darkness upon the face of the deep."

Black holes were first discovered because of their incredibly bright x-ray emissions, signaling the greatest destructive processes in the universe.[15] If a large black hole forms in an area of space with lots of matter on which to feed, or if two or more black holes coalesce into one, black holes may become huge and incredibly destructive, and with enough material-input they may even become "supermassive." Astronomers have surmised the existence of a supermassive black hole called *the "Great Attractor,"* which is gravitationally powerful enough to tug thousands of galaxies and galaxy clusters in its direction—one of which is our own Milky Way. Recently, the existence of a far more massive black hole has also been surmised, an object which may, in fact, be controlling the movement of the Great Attractor and several others like it! What lies at and beyond (above) this level in the hierarchy of black holes is anyone's guess! My father always said that if something swims, has feathers and "quacks," we should call it a duck! The movement of galaxies, galaxy-groups, and supermassive black holes suggests all sorts of "feathers," "quacks," and soft ducky down. In more scientific terms, we can see evidence of what lies ahead in what has already occurred. The notion of a Big Crunch is sustained by all of this—by: (1) a *system or hierarchy of increasingly colossal black holes* that control increasingly larger segments of the universe, and (2) observable, evolutionary processes by which virtually all black holes are able to grow in size and potency.

In addition to this, within the past few decades evidence has been mounting that: (a) black holes are *the* attractive forces lurking at the centers of galaxies, binding the galaxies together, and (b) black holes are to galaxies as a sun is to a solar system—which is to say that there is a direct relationship between the size of a galaxy or galaxy cluster and the size of its centralized black hole. This, upon reflection, becomes a very profound relationship suggesting not only that big galaxies are driven by large black holes, but also that galaxy **clusters** are driven by supermassive black holes, and huge galaxy clusters are driven by "colossal" black holes. *The incredible size of some of galaxy clusters suggests that the "Great Attractor" indeed has a colossal grandfather, and that "ol' granddad" may only be a start to what we shall ultimately find out in the distant recesses of space! How far Ol' Granddad is from the top of the hierarchy is an issue* *that we can only speculate about, and study.* However, Martin Rees is among many noted astrophysicists who openly suggest that black holes may have been involved in the collapse of one or more pre-existing universes.

So, there is physical evidence that black holes are constantly devouring more and more matter, with some achieving supermassive and even colossal size, in which case they are capable of devouring ever-greater successions of galaxy clusters, other colossal black holes, and perhaps ultimately the universe, itself. But then what? Scientists have long debated whether the universe would ever emerge from such a grand kaput. Interestingly, Stephen Hawking has offered a theory suggesting that even black holes can self-destruct, which means that they might not constitute the final resting place of matter, after all. As reckoned by Hawking, the time required for this process would be a bit mind-boggling (the actual number of years is mathematically expressed as 1×10^{66}, which can be written as a 1 followed by a staggering 66 zeroes.[16] For matter (or a universe) in an omega state, however, time would have no relevance. Hawking's theory borrows from active processes occurring along the periphery of all black holes. It suggests that as *matter approaches the "event horizon" of a black hole (the point past which nothing can return), it becomes progressively compressed, heated and irradiated. As this process continues, infalling matter begins to give off bursts of very high-energy radiation. The collision of high-energy radiation beams would then produce matter in the form of electrons, and antimatter in the form of positrons, and these would instantaneously annihilate each other. In this super-catastrophic environment, immense amounts of "virtual" (force-producing) particles would be produced, and then fall into the black hole. While virtual particles have no mass, they carry the great forces of nature and therefore act upon the mass of the black hole—the result being a kind of "negative energy," which (under the laws of relativity) spells negative mass. So, Hawking's theory implies a steady reduction in the physical size of the black hole. The black hole would shrink a bit with each virtual particle input, just as if it were spewing a steady stream of matter into space.*

At some stage in this process, subatomic particles would begin to be released from compression, and the internal temperature of the black hole would skyrocket. Precarious instability would follow, followed very soon by a tremendous nuclear explosion—perhaps a "Big Bang." Hawking ("A Brief History..." p. 107) in no way contends that our universe began with an explosion of a super-colossal black hole, but the potential application of his theory is obvious. In Hawking's own words:

> Moreover, the lower the mass of the black hole, the higher its temperature. So as the black hole loses mass, its temperature and rate of emission increase, so it loses mass more quickly. What happens when the mass of the black hole eventually becomes extremely small is not quite clear, but the most reasonable guess is that it would disappear completely in a tremendous final burst of emission, equivalent to the explosion of millions of H-bombs.[17]

A few billion years after this sort of hypothetical "Big Bang" might have created a universe, intelligent lifeforms arguing about the nature of the universe might arise and invent something called science. Then, sometime later, trained "scientists" would come along and develop something called astronomy, and these "astronomers" would ultimately observe a great outrushing of matter, as if from some hypothetical centralized point-of-explosion. A few of them would soon agree on the term "Hubble Flow" to describe this phenomenon. Some would then investigate the possibility that the Hubble Flow was beginning to ebb, perhaps due to the gravitational attraction of the universe, itself.

To evaluate this important issue, a group of super-intelligent astronomers called *"astrophysicists"* would one day step from the shadows, clean off their dusty monocles, and coin two very divergent models of eternity: (1) that of an "OPEN" universe, and (2) that of a "CLOSED" universe. The universe would be termed "open" if its total mass were found to be gravitationally insufficient to stop the outrushing of matter from the Big Bang. In such a universe, galaxies would perpetually move farther and farther apart. *Over time*, the great nuclear furnaces of the stars would be spread thin and thinner. At last, perhaps after hundreds of billions of years, there would come a time when the last star in the universe had burned itself out, when matter would be spread so thin that basic atomic energy levels would begin to fizzle, when everything would become bleak and dark and utterly cold—a universe of desolate, floating, useless, burned-out cinders.

The model of a "closed" universe offers an entirely different end-scenario—here, the force of gravity becomes strong enough to halt the outward expansion of the universe, and ultimately drags all matter back to the point of origin. Collapse soon creates a dense cloud of intermingled matter, growing in heat as atoms increasingly collide and atomic reactions occur. Eventually, the center of this great collapsing mass bursts into a stupendous sea of fire and radiation. It is the Big Bang, in reverse. Ultimately, as collapse continues, everything is snuffed out, the alpha-phase universe ceases to be, and all matter is zipped into a colossal black hole. Nothing is left but an invisible black hole, the void, and a cold, quiet, perpetually foreboding "darkness upon the face of the deep."

The significance of all this for *The God Theory* is that these two alternative models of the universe offer profoundly differing views of "eternity." If the universe is *closed*, gravity, operative through black holes and "dark matter," becomes an *eternal driving force*, operative in both the alpha and the omega universe. Over enormous stretches of time, the matter and energy of creation is relentlessly driven into and out of colossal black holes. A living universe is born from the explosion of a colossal black hole, and then dies in gravitational collapse as a similar black hole is ultimately reformed. Alternatively, if the universe is *open*, it explodes into being (for reasons unknown), eternally expands, then someday runs out of energy, fizzles and ceases to be relevant. A *closed universe*, despite its accompanying destructive horror, implies eternal rebirth and regeneration, and hope. An open universe, on the other hand, implies little more than a final flicker, infinite darkness, and nothing more, forever.

Science has yet to prove either model, and is still offering new ones that are of little concern here. Suffice it to say that most calculations have heretofore indicated that there is insufficient baryonic (normal) matter in the universe to harness and reverse the expansion of the galaxies, and close the universe. Thus, during most of the 20th Century astronomers have generally theorized that the galaxies would continue to move farther and farther apart, and hence that the universe would ultimately evolve into a state of lifelessness and utter desolation. However, during the final third of the 20th Century, evidence has slowly accumulated in support of the notion of a "closed" universe:

> So much still lies out there unseen. Only recently have we begun to glimpse the lumpy nature of the large-scale structure of the universe. In 1989, astronomers Margaret Geller and John Huchra of the Harvard-Smithsonian Center for Astrophysics confirmed, after plotting thousands of galaxies into a three-dimensional map, that most galaxies are clustered in sheets. In between those sheets lie voids—vast bubbles of apparent nothingness.
> We have, moreover, realized that the Milky Way, our entire Local Group (of galaxies), and thousands of other galaxies in our vicinity are being pulled at about 360 miles a second toward a huge concentration of galactic matter called the Great Attractor, whose tug indicates it has the mass of about 20,000 trillion suns. "More recently we've discovered that even the Great Attractor is in motion, perhaps drawn toward something with as much as ten times more mass. We are thus like rafts on a cosmic river, streaming toward the unknown.[18]

The living universe is responding to the growing "omega

universe," and there are hints that black holes are not the only forms of dark matter in existence. Stars in a neighboring galaxy, the "Large Magellanic Cloud," for example, move with velocities that could only be produced by something with five to ten times more mass than the observable matter of our entire galaxy and surrounding regions of space.[19] Moreover, the ROSAT international satellite has detected a vast cloud of ionized gas enshrouding three galaxies known as the NGC 2300 Group, and "that cloud," explains astronomer David Burstein of Arizona State University, "is much too immense for the group to gravitationally hold on to—unless the group has 15 to 25 times more mass than we can see."[20]

So, what is dark matter?! One of the most burning issues in astrophysics, today—is the form, or various forms, of dark matter. Theories portend that this mysterious stuff may take a variety of forms, accounting for perhaps as much as 99 percent of the mass of the entire universe. Martin Rees of Cambridge University recently went on record affirming (in quite an understatement) that black holes are now considered to be "*possible* candidates for the dark matter in galaxies..."[21] But obviously, there are others. Some scientists believe that dark matter is nothing exotic or hypothetical, and that most of it simply consists of unseen, burned-out stars known as "white dwarfs." Others favor more exotic explanations, and suggest that there are many forms other than black holes.

Dark matter, in reality, is not the central issue in the debate over whether the universe is open or closed. The real underlying, central issue is the mass of the universe, and whether the mass is sufficient to cause it to gravitationally close. One problem we have in dealing with this issue is the state of science, and what we don't yet know about the universe. Recent findings about the tiny "*neutrino*" highlight this issue. The precise nature of the neutrino has been a source of controversy for decades. Questions about the possible mass of the neutrino have long been deemed significant, since neutrinos are known to be omnipresent and in plentiful supply throughout the universe. Neutrinos have sometimes been described in popular magazines as "ghostly particles" due to their unique ability to slip, unscathed, through atoms and sub-atomic particles. Experiments have shown them to be so tiny as to be able to travel through *an entire planet* without even being deflected due to a chance sub-atomic collision. Until the last decade of the 20th Century, some physicists believed that neutrinos were, in fact, *virtual particles*, i.e. particles without mass delivering only the forces of nature. Others argued that they were *real particles*, with mass, and that their mass might well add just enough additional mass to the estimated mass of the universe to confirm the model of a closed universe.

The neutrino was first conceptualized by Wolfgang Pauli, in 1930, in an effort to explain minute energy losses in nuclear reactions. Pauli believed that the neutrino had practically no mass at all, but he was never able to prove its existence and determine its precise nature. It was not until 1994 that physicists Frederick Reines and Clyde Cowan confirmed that the neutrino existed (a feat for which they received the 1995 Nobel Prize in Physics). The nature and outcome of their experiments strongly suggested that the neutrino was a "real particle"—a particle with mass, occupying space. However, it was left to Japanese scientists to confirm this in an important 1998 finding—contained in the "Official Super-Kamiokande Press Release" of June 5, 1998, as follows:

> The new evidence is based upon studies of neutrinos which are created when cosmic rays, fast-moving particles from space, bombard the earth's upper atmosphere producing cascades of secondary particles which rain down upon the earth. Most of these neutrinos pass through the entire earth unscathed... Faint flashes of light given off by the neutrino interactions in the chemically- doctored gathering) tank are detected by more than 13,000 photomultiplier tubes...
>
> By classifying the neutrino interactions according to the type of neutrino involved (electron-neutrino or muon-neutrino) and counting their relative numbers as a function of the distance from their creation point, we

conclude that the muon-neutrinos are 'oscillating'. Oscillation is the changing back and forth of a neutrino's type as it travels through space or matter. This can occur only if the neutrino possesses mass...[22]

The muon neutrino, as an incessant product of the nuclear reactions of stars and other phenomena, now comes to us as a new source of matter to be factored into estimates of the total amount of matter in the universe. The nature and possible mass of the "electron neutrino" remain at issue for further study. An important point is that as we grow in knowledge, new variables always appear that have to be factored into the equations. Because this factoring process is never quite complete, the various models of our universe are never quite perfect.

Is this added mass of the tiny neutrino enough to cause the universe to close? We simply don't yet know. Some astrophysicists suggest that dark matter is enough, and that if dark matter—whatever its form—accounts for as much as 70 to 80 percent of the universe, the Hubble Flow will necessarily someday ebb, the galaxies will begin to close, and the universe will eventually die in a fit of radiation, fire and gravitational collapse, as follows (Jastrow):

....If the pull of gravity is sufficiently strong, it may bring the expansion (of our universe) to a halt at some point in the future. "What will happen then? The answer is the crux of this theory. The elements of the Universe, held in a balance between the outward momentum of the primordial explosion and the inward force of gravity, stand momentarily at rest; but after the briefest instant, always drawn together by gravity, they commence to move toward one another. Slowly at first, and then with increasing momentum, the Universe collapses under the relentless pull of gravity. Soon the galaxies of the Cosmos rush toward one another with an inward movement as violent as the outward movement of their expansion when the Universe exploded earlier. After a sufficient time, they come into contact; their gases mix; their atoms are heated by compression; and the Universe returns to the heat and chaos from which it emerged many billions of years ago.

And after that? No one knows. Some astronomers say the Universe will never come out of this collapsed state. Others speculate that the Universe will rebound from the collapse in a new explosion, and experience a new moment of Creation. According to this view, our Universe will be melted down and remade in the caldron of the second creation. It will become an entirely new world, in which no trace of the existing Universe remains.[23]

Astrophysicist George Greenstein presents a colorful (and more frightening) view of the same culminating events in *The Symbiotic Universe*, p. 130-131:

What is the ultimate fate of the expansion? One possibility is that in the long run it will reverse. Untold ages hence, in an evolution vast, ponderous, and majestic, the galaxies' outward motion will slow to a halt. Briefly—"briefly" in cosmic terms—they will hover. And then, slowly at first but with ever increasing speed, they will plummet together.

When the overall scale of the universe has contracted by a factor of fifty, the galaxies will merge... The nighttime sky in those far distant epochs will be spectacularly beautiful as a multitude of stars... mingle together. New constellations will appear in the heavens. At the same time, however, winters will begin to grow uncommonly mild, summers uncommonly severe. A new form of heat will be flooding down—heat not from the Sun, but from the universe itself.

...As the universe continues contracting it will grow sufficiently hot that oceans will boil. The background radiation will gradually shift to a sullen, deep-red glow, ominously filling the nighttime sky as it pours down upon us. As the contraction proceeds the radiation will grow brighter and shift in color up the spectrum, ultimately reaching a hideous electric blue. Under its awful heat rocks will melt, the surface of the Earth grow molten—and then grow hotter still, the very planet itself vaporizing, dissolving into the fire. The same will be the fate of every other body in the universe... The storm of that destruction will be a mirror image of the fires of our birth, the Big Bang in which the universe began so many eons ago.[24]

And now for the punch line—the New Testament, 2nd Peter 3:10, also describes the end of time—in words that are not dissimilar to those of Jastrow and Greenstein:

10 But the day of the Lord will come as a thief in the night, *in which the heavens will pass away with a great noise, and the elements will melt with fervent heat; both the earth and the works that are in it will be burned up.*[25]

The Bible, in other words, makes its own predictions about the end of time, predictions that seem to parallel those of Einstein and other scientists. So, can it possibly be that what the scriptures are talking about is nothing more than the paradigm of a "closed," oscillating universe? This raises an even bigger question—do parallels between science and scripture suggest that both may have a single source? Something very profound has happened during this analogy, and it should not be overlooked. The biblical doomsday has been connected with the notion of a closed universe, which is itself connected to the hierarchy of black holes and dark matter in our universe. Scripture, in other words, is making predictions that are substantiated by facts and phenomena that we can observe in the everyday universe. Feynmann called this "truth," and Deuteronomy tells us that truth is always *of God*. So, in studying science, have we not enhanced the credibility of the Bible and strengthened the case for the age-old doctrine of "divine inspiration"? And does divine inspiration suggest that there is a "Divine"?

Such findings as this are only part of the rationale for the "new synthesis." Correlation of science and scripture is significant and substantive, suggesting that composite paradigms of the two may well be valid. We will never know, of course, until we build such composites and put them to the test, and, of course, I plan to do precisely that in successive chapters.

We have found in this chapter that *composites of science and scripture can be constructed which contribute important new meaning to age-old mysteries. In the foregoing chapters, we found that large portions of Genesis seem to have human rather than divine inspiration, because God can never be the author of error.* The only possible conclusion we can draw from this is that God has given us "Divine Revelation," but we have inevitably added our own observations and conclusions—and perhaps occasionally we have either corrupted His Word or made it less believable. This can occur because of overt editing, but, as shown in the foregoing chapters, it can also occur via misinterpretation. And there have certainly been human interpretive masterpieces such as geocentrism, heavenly H_2O and other portions of the Ptolemaic Model of the Universe.

If a Deity exists, He truly planted the seeds of science as well as scripture in the creative fires of the Big Bang, and the flowering of both was just as pre-ordained (in generality), as the current, observable state of our physical universe. As this chapter suggests, a number of other events are also pre-ordained, including a coming doomsday, and a new creation. Do these imply the existence of God, or simply the existence of great eternal cycles of creation and destruction? Is our view of eternity to be prevailingly Judeo-Christian, or prevailingly Hindu-Buddhist? And could it be that none of these models are quite adequate?

While there has recently been an accumulation of hard and theoretical evidence in favor of a closed universe, there is still insufficient evidence to exclude other models from the realm of possibility. Comparatively recent findings, in fact, seem to have given new life to the paradigm of an *open universe*. Supernovae, for example, are well known for their constant, predictable levels of luminescence, and are thus a dependable favorite of astronomers in establishing the distance, speed and direction-of-movement of objects at very great distance from the Earth. The Hubble Telescope has implicitly made it possible to observe and study such objects in detail. These observations have shown an increasing red-shift with increasing distance from the Earth, as expected, *but recent findings on the extent of that red-shift have been entirely unexpected! These have found that the most distant observable supernovae* are, in fact, about twenty percent more red-shifted than expected. Many astronomers interpret this as an overt acceleration of matter along the edge of the universe. If such an acceleration is ultimately proven, models of a closed universe would be completely contravened, for the paradigm of a closed universe inherently suggests that matter should be *decelerating* with increasing distance in space from the point of the initial explosion.

A problem with these supernovae studies is the space-time continuum, itself, which creates major interpretive problems across the vast distances of interstellar space. In looking at an object five billion light years distant, we are essentially seeing it as it was five billion years ago. Its light is five billion years old and has taken five billion years to reach us. A primary tenet of the Big Bang Theory, inflation, suggests that the Big Bang hurled virtual particles across space at many times the speed of light prior to condensation of real particles from the fires of the explosion. At condensation, real particles were being propelled by waning inflation (and indirectly by the explosion's force) at uncanny speeds. Thus, all the matter of the universe was once outrushing at a much faster velocity than now. Could it be, then, that what we are actually witnessing is the higher post-inflationary velocities of the primordial galaxies? Might this additional 20% red-shift simply be a product of the universe's inflation, eons ago? Because of a plethora of uncertainties about this phenomenon, it is far too early for scientists to announce hard findings of fact. Problems in interpretation of red-shift measurements across the space-time continuum, in the face of many other unknowns, is reason enough for scientists to be timid while the investigation continues.

The fact of the matter is that science has not yet established the ultimate fate of the universe. The Bible, on the other hand, is quite clear about the events that are to come, and it makes several direct assertions to the effect that the universe will someday be physically destroyed in a cataclysmic doomsday event. The Book of Second Peter specifically tells us that the universe will die in "fervent heat," and then Revelation adds mention of a "lake of fire" after a final judgment. Finally, it speaks of the creation of a new heaven and new Earth:

> And I (John) saw a new heaven and a new earth, for the first heaven and the first earth had passed away. Also there was no more sea. (Revelation 21:1)

All of this seems to endorse the scenario of a closed-universe and a second round of creation—support for the notion of an "oscillating" universe—a universe that expires in a penultimate gravitational collapse, but then is reborn and recreated. Chapter 21 of Revelation finally adds moral intent—The Almighty removes imperfection via the destruction of our existing universe, and then creates a better one " ...in which righteousness dwells."

The composite of science and scripture thus affirms the existence of a great superstructure and a wheel of eternity—great caissons that roll forever between the alpha and the omega. The force of gravity always provides the propulsion, and The Almighty sparks the fires of creation. The Bible tells us that one of God's purposes in all of this is to achieve perfection. We will save further discussion of the "whys" for the final chapter.

As an earth scientist, I find biblical confirmation of a new Earth—"without seas"—profound, for I know that our own Earth, initially after its formation, had no seas. A new Earth without seas coming down out of heaven is thus an appropriate prophetic vision. It tells of something that happened previously. An essential point is that profound paradigms such as this stem from the "composite" of science and scripture. Literalism leaves us only with abject confusion. The correlation of science and scripture that facilitates these composites inevitably suggests that everything emanates from a single source, and that the universe is truly one.

CHAPTER THREE

THE DOORSTEP OF GOD

For reasons expressed in the previous chapter, a major premise of the *God Theory*, is a simple assertion that the universe is closed and oscillating. The evidence for this oscillating eternity is found in both science and scripture. Scripture tells us that the universe will die in heat and fire, and that there will be a wonderful new beginning. Science suggests that we came into being as a result of a "Big Bang" and that we are inevitably headed for a "Big Crunch." A universe of great complexity exits between these two events. Science is only capable of dealing with events confined to the "alpha universe," but scripture is capable of dealing with both the alpha and the omega sides of creation.

This chapter will demonstrate that the Bible contains profound references to the omega universe that are sometimes profoundly hidden. It will also show how biblical literalism can *deprive* us of a significant understanding of the universe and eternity. Conversely, the available information about both is maximized in the ***composite*** of science and scripture. Once we lift the veil of literalism from Genesis and become sensitive and anticipative of events uniquely described by science, we can literally peer into the portals of eternity. What we find on the other side of the door of creation is an omega-phase "proto-universe" that contains observable features and real physical substance. It is described in the simple language of Genesis 1:2:

> 2. And the earth was without form and void; and darkness was upon THE FACE of the deep, and the

spirit of God moved across THE FACE of the waters.

Building on the analogies of the last chapter, the phrases "without form and void," and "darkness was upon the face of the deep," would seem to imply the existence of a supercolossal black hole containing a complete omega-phase universe. The phrase "face of the deep" suggests an environment like that of space, and the phrase "face of the waters" comes to us as a subtle affirmation of the Ptolemaic model, but one which also signals the existence of matter. Genesis is setting the stage, here, for creation of an alpha-phase universe, and God is about to become a party-to and a participant-in a series of definitive pre-creational events.

We know that this "pre-creational environment" contained MATTER because of the repeated use of the term "face," in addition to the mention of the term "waters." Only a material object can have a definable "face." The term "face" also allows us to effectively distinguish an hypothesized black hole from the relatively empty and "deep" void of space. There are, in other words, discernible objects. We can only establish the proper context for what is occurring via a sneak reading of Genesis 1:3, which suggests an impending explosion that will create LIGHT—the light of a future living universe, *light that will transform the impenetrable darkness of a cold and desolate* **pit** *into a* **place** *of warmth and incredible beauty.*

In the interpretation that spins from a composite of science and scripture a view of creation emerges that is sharply divergent from the traditional. *In Chapter One of this book we noted that the traditional (Ptolemaic or pre-Copernican) interpretation of Genesis is rooted in the theology of the Babylonian captivity. The term "waters," in the Ptolemaic world referenced real, liquid waters within a separate sphere, surrounding a* **tiny, domelike universe** *that enclosed the Earth. This interpretation allowed that water could either fall from the sky or bubble-up from beneath a decidedly* **flat Earth**. The archaic references are hard for us to understand. The term "earth" was synonymous with "ground," and the word "heavens" was synonymous with "air." It was believed that angels dwelled within the sphere of heavens (air) that lay above the pre-creational waters and the flat but formless, pre-creational land. God, of course, was free to enter any realm of the universe and observe, a view apparent from the literal words of Genesis 1:2, in which it seemed only logical (to ancient clerics) that someone standing on the "pre-creational ground" at the time of creation, and looking upwards, might have been able to see God moving across (or upon) the face of the heavenly (Ptolemaic) waters just prior to the appearance of light. The great theologian John Calvin (like many others of his day) actually believed that the sky derived its blue color from these heavenly waters. This was a notion derived from the "Ptolemaic Model," and thus traceable to the ancient Middle East.

Imagine a child, today, with questions about the validity of the Bible, listening to a Sunday School teacher touting the notion of heavenly waters above the sky, as if this were the literal truth of God! Which is the real sin—incorrect and fallacious teachings based on literalism and ancient ignorance, or the injection of "real" and proven knowledge into scriptural interpretation? Fundamentalists would have us believe that an accurate translation of the Bible, predicated at least partially on science, is somehow sinful. Yet, a typical 5th grader, today, knows the basic nature of the universe, and understands some of the most fundamental laws of chemistry and physics. He/she knows, for example, that light waves can be bent through a prism to produce a rainbow. The story of Noah, however, requires him/her to reject that knowledge in favor of the biblical assertion that God sent the rainbow for the first time ever, to Noah, as a reminder of His Promise that the Earth would never again be completely flooded. In truth, the literal Genesis is full of such perversions and contradictions of reality. Because they cannot be supported by observation of the real world, we can use the rule of Feynmann and Deuteronomy to declare them pointedly false. They are human creations, and not of God. Are we to expect our own children to believe that light was somehow different before the time of Noah? Were the antediluvian light waves somehow less bendable, so that prisms could not have performed the same work as now?

Babylonian mythology, human double-distillation and ancient bad science has given the Old Testament a host of problems that can only be resolved by laying waste to biblical literalism. This does not mean that Bibles should be burned, or that we should strain over the meaning of every scriptural phrase to guarantee scientific precision, it means that the 21st Century world should not be ruled by the logic of 1,000 B.C. It means that 21st Century knowledge should be used to interpret the circumstances of the ancient world, while understanding the perspective, the limited world view and the prevailing ignorance of the ancients. We call this process colligation, and it can greatly assist in an understanding of events such as "Noah's Flood." An abundance of archaeological and geological evidence, for example, does confirm the occurrence of a great flood, but shows that it was nowhere near worldwide in proportion, as stated by Genesis. Modern efforts to examine the Black Sea basin have found the waters of that basin to contain a proliferation of freshwater fossil species, and thus far these have been dated at between 7,500 and 15,500 years in age. At about 6,800 years ago, however, saltwater species suddenly appear. This finding clearly signals that the Black Sea was once a freshwater lake—a lake flooded by the Mediterranean after the collapse of a natural dam about 7,000 years ago. Relict beaches and human artifacts along ancient submerged shorelines, more than 500 ft beneath the surface of the modern Black Sea testify to the validity of that theory. Set in proper historical and physiological context, 20,000 years ago the sea level was about 120 meters lower than it is today. As the last great ice age ended, the seas began to rise. A land bridge probably existed at this time joining modern day Greece and Turkey across the Bhosporus Straits. The precise nature of this land bridge cannot now be determined. It may have been an area of rubble deposited by glaciers, a low-lying portion of the continental shelf, or it may simply have been an area of structural weakness due to incessant movement of area tectonic plates. Whatever the nature of this land bridge, it separated the salty waters of the rising Mediterranean from the fresh waters of the relatively low-lying Black Sea. After a time, perhaps an earthquake or maybe just the growing pressure of a rising Mediterranean, caused the failure of this land bridge. As a result, an avalanche of saltwater was sent cascading into the lower-lying basin. The resulting flood lasted not 40 days, but approximately 40 years. Noah may very well have been a real person who lived along the banks of that ancient freshwater lake, who saw its waters rapidly overflowing their banks, and who thought that God was truly destroying the entire world—no one knows, of course. What *is* clear is that the flood was geographically limited in scope, and that there would have been no reason for God to send lions, tigers, elephants, hippopotami, etc., to Noah for boarding onto an "Ark." If animals were herded onto an "Ark," they were most likely Noah's own farm animals.

"Noah's Flood" always stimulates considerable debate among biblical scholars. Because there is an account of a great flood in Mesopotamian mythology, which seems to be older than the story of Noah, many scholars believe that Noah is simply a Hebrew adaptation of the Mesopotamian tale. Mesopotamian mythology may therefore have entered the Hebrew scriptures during the Babylonian captivity—a time of intense and prolonged contact between the Hebrew and Chaldean cultures. While prose may seem to ascribe the story to the Yahwist tradition, there are significant historical reasons to believe otherwise. The scope of this "great flood" is also at issue. Some noted scholars (Dr. Gerald Schroeder, among them) discount traditional assertions that the flood was worldwide in scope, and suggest that a more accurate translation of the Hebrew text limits the expanse of the flood to the "known world," or a "defined region."

But, to me, the story of Noah provides a very important case-in-point of the implicit harm in literalism. If the story is taken literally, we must ultimately believe that thousands of animals lived comfortably aboard a craft that could have accommodated no more than a few hundred, that the flood was caused by the waters of *outer space* breaking through a glasslike shell separating them from our atmosphere, and that God afterwards gave us a rainbow to mark His promise that there will never be another flood, and that rainbows did not exist before the great flood. On every single issue, moreover, the story fails and becomes a fiasco that is not believable. On the other hand, the story of Noah and the Ark can be taken for what it most likely is—a parable, a simple story based perhaps upon shreds of truth, but expanded upon and used by the Hebrew Priests of Babylon to illustrate the great power and potentially horrible wrath of God. Hebrew priests frequently taught in parables, and used them as powerful vehicles for securing obedience to Jewish laws. It is not that those priests were liars. To them, the story of Noah and the Ark was plausible given their state of scientific knowledge, but the key idea is that they didn't really care whether it was plausible, or not, because it was simply a teaching tool. It presented the notion of a wrathful, raging deity—the same sort of God Who had allowed the Babylonians to overrun and destroy the sinful Nation of Judah. It was the very antithesis of the parable of the "Prodigal Son" recounted by Jesus in the New Testament, telling us that God destroys, while the prodigal son tells us that God forgives. A central problem with the Old Testament is that time, scriptural revision and human double-distillation has frequently washed away intent and purpose, and confused the truth.

The biblical book of Daniel (Chapter One to be precise), directly asserts that select Hebrew men were taken to the court of Nebuchadnezzar to learn the arts (and sciences) of the Chaldeans (i.e. Babylonians). Daniel and others among those selected for this educational experience ultimately became leaders of the Jewish nation in exile. The Book of Daniel therefore provides *direct* confirmation that Babylonian culture and myth was assimilated into Judaism. Since the Hebrew Priests of Babylon revised, abridged and thoroughly rewrote much of Genesis during their exile, the probability that the Jews assimilated significant Chaldean culture is virtually 100 percent. Taught in the context of a parable, the story of Noah comes to us as a colorful and fascinating illustration of the consequences of sin. Taught as literal truth, however, it collapses for lack of reason and logical/ historical support. The impact of such a collapse on one's faith, however, can be catastrophic! The only way we can deal effectively with this is to remember that human "double-distillation" is not *God's fault! If we are to seek unadulterated Divine Revelation, the most logical place to look is in portions of the Bible where the possibility of editing has been minimized.* The original Yahwist creation story (appearing principally in the 2nd and 3rd Chapters of Genesis) seems to have been spared significant editing, and it is far less paradoxical than the account that was written on or about 560 B.C., in Babylon.

Today, the general nature of the universe is pretty much a done deal. The first telescopes, and certainly the first Sputnik, affirmed once and for all that there are no liquid waters within a separate sphere above the atmosphere, and no hardshell firmament separating heavenly waters from an *"underlying"* sky! The Ptolemaic view of the universe is obviously incorrect! Why then should anyone continue to embrace a biblical literalism that separates God from this world? The central reason, I believe, is fear. Many theologians are afraid that if one tiny phrase of scripture is disavowed due to error, all of it might ultimately go crashing down, and so they have become trapped by their own insecurity into shoring up an indefensible belief system. In an important sense, such problems are an inevitable result of trying to set the Bible on a reverential plane with God, and having the Bible or some holy book as one's only source of faith. The fact of the matter is that the Bible is just a collection of documents written by men about God, and it doesn't deserve a Divine status. It didn't float down to us from heaven, as we have noted before. That it has been increasingly given a divine status is, in large part, a result of the fervor of theologians for "Divine and absolute Truth." And commonfolk will certainly listen to what is identified as "God's Word," in church, easier than they will Tolstoy's *War and Peace*, or Shakespeare's *MacBeth*. Identifying something as "God's Word" imparts credibility on the one interpreting that word and delivering it as a sermon or lesson. *Yet, true Divine Revelation would never attempt to force us into believing something that can be proven untrue!*

In promulgating that which is untrue simply because it is part of "God's Word," the credibility of many fundamentalist theologians ultimately suffers. The problems of fundamentalism stem not only from a misunderstanding and ignorance of science, but also from a general misunderstanding of the historical and cultural basis of the Old Testament. As a result, many of the stories of the Old and New Testament are misinterpreted. A classic example of this is provided by Bishop John Shelby Spong (*Rescuing the Bible from Fundamentalism*), in a discussion about the story of Ruth. Spong recounts that at the time the Book of Ruth was written, Jewish religious leaders believed that *all* of the prior sufferings of the Nation of Israel had occurred because of the ethnic and cultural intermixing of their forefathers with the non-Jewish peoples of ancient Palestine. Thus, laws had been passed, and were enforced via penalties of banishment and/or death, prohibiting a non-Jew from living in Judah, and all Jews were prohibited from marrying anyone who was not a full-blooded Jew to the tenth-generation.

These laws were so strong, so popularly supported and so rigorously enforced that they could not be openly opposed. To attempt to do so would result in immediate banishment or death. Even in this radical and dangerous climate, however, a brave rabbi and scribe arose in opposition to the evils of ethnic cleansing and created the story of Ruth. Ruth, of course, was a Moabite woman married to a Jew. She was a woman who not only adopted Jewish ways, but who remained faithful to her Jewish mother-in-law even after the untimely death of her husband. She truly became a model of goodness and loyalty, and took on the highest cultural aspirations of Judaism and the Hebrew people. Most importantly, as Spong notes, Ruth mothered Obed, who fathered Jesse, who, in turn, fathered King David. In the end, the story of Ruth hammers home a thunderbolt—*King David, himself—the greatest, most exalted, and most beloved of all Hebrew kings—was, in fact, a person of mixed ancestry!* Thus, under the laws operative at the time the story of Ruth was written, King David, of all people, would have been among those exiled, banished and/or killed! A literal interpretation of Ruth is completely blind to this historical and cultural setting, and totally misses the point of the fantastic broadside against tyranny that is contained within Ruth!

The typical fundamentalist lesson associated with the story of Ruth is one that exalts the decency, faithfulness and sacrifice of a virtuous woman. It is a message that is, at very best, only partially correct.

The truth is that literalism has twisted our theology into a weakened superstructure that is about to collapse under its own weight. The supreme and central paradox of literalism is that it ultimately requires us to believe that an OMNISCIENT God either knew not the precise nature of His own Creation, or lied to us; or that He handed the world over to the Devil and has since allowed Satan to rule and deceive us to his heart's content! This goes directly counter to the Bible, which repeatedly asserts that God is the Creator of *all* things and the Master of the universe. Clearly, literalists have painted themselves into a corner. I do not intend, by any means, to infer that all applications of literalism are bad, my point is simply that literalism misapplied is dangerous and can transform God into the author and supreme architect of error and idiocy! Idiocy, however, belongs to men and not God. If there truly is a God, He does not deserve such a legacy and we should give Him the reverence and respect that He truly deserves! We can only do that by stirring modern science into theology.

Someday, in the far distant future, human occupants of spaceships escaping our solar system will see the Earth shrink, grow tiny, and eventually disappear into the glare of the sun. A few hundred years later, as descendants of these same astronauts approach a distant star, they will witness our own sun shrink and eventually fade into the backdrop of the Milky Way. Even their most powerful optical telescopes will not enable them to view the Earth from this faraway location. They will be alone and surrounded by a vast universe. The notion of a tiny astrodome-type universe centered about a tiny Earth and surrounded by heavenly waters—*an idea (and a place) attributable only to ancient mythology*—will surely evoke chuckles, head shaking, and absolute disavowal! These futuristic explorers and space colonizers will be seeing the universe first-hand, as it truly is—incredibly vast, incredibly beautiful, with immense resources. They will know beyond doubt that the universe is so large that most of it will NEVER be accessible to even the fastest of human starships! How, then, can we expect such people to accept worship that endorses a God in the sky who looks down and watches over all of us, through *heavenly H_2O*, and who rules from the separate sphere of heaven within the geocentric model of a tiny universe?

The problems of the "LITERAL" Bible combined with an archaic theology are literally overwhelming! But how does one realistically hope to escape literalism's intricate, traditional theological web of medieval science and psychology? How does one dismantle literalism, and its evils without throwing the baby out with the bathwater—without discarding all of the good (believe it or not) that can also be found in fundamentalism? It is not my desire to torpedo the scriptures, or the good, "God-fearing" fundamentalists. My plain and simple desire is to dramatically shift the focus of Judeo-Christian theology—to move it light years forward into an open embrace of proven scientific truths so that it can be truly appropriate for what lies ahead.

Scriptural and scientific truths need to be served to us on the same plate, if we are to swallow anything—if we are truly to understand the mysteries of God, Creation and our own being. To find and explain God, we must find a consistent means of sifting through, analyzing and merging the grand truths of the universe, be they scientific or scriptural. Fortunately, there is a systematic theological means of doing this. In reviewing the works of natural theologians and scientists, and relevant comments about deity and creation, it becomes clear that what we are really being presented with, in a sense, is two sets of scriptures—*one written (and sometimes edited and distilled) by human hands, the other embellished by God across the grand face of the heavens and the entire universe!* Ours is the prerogative of accepting either of these, or both. We can use what God has created to shape our scriptural interpretation and to correct the errors of human double-distillation. This means that we must comprehensively understand the natural universe, the proven body of scientific knowledge, and the scientific method.

Accepting science as a universal standard for scriptural

interpretation will certainly roll some eyeballs! At the very least, it will require us to develop and embrace *a comprehensive "Neo-Natural Theology"! It will require theologians to recognize that nothing is inherently wrong in using science to promulgate a rational view of God and Creation. Rationalizing the scriptures will, in fact, eliminate paradox and make the scriptures dynamic, more believable, and intimately relevant! Staying with literalism will only perpetuate an incorrect view of the universe and God, and undermine the credibility of theology insofar as future generations are concerned. We really have no choice!*

A guiding philosophy for integrating science and theology might be termed **"scriptural dynamism."** Scriptural dynamism is implicit in the *God Theory* and tells us that an active God used active **"processes"** (not magic) to bring about creation! It fundamentally tells us that the heavens and the Earth contain the handwriting and signature of the Creator, and that Feynmann's notion of observable truths should be our guide in scripture as well as science. Yet, because the scriptures recount many historical events that cannot be observed, tested and evaluated, the application of scriptural dynamism must be limited to events about which there is hard evidence and/or credible theory—as in the creation (i.e. the Big Bang). Scriptural dynamism will also give us a consistent, accurate means for filling in scriptural holes with proven scientific knowledge, and/or accepted theories. This will not be a panacea, and there will be problems, but it beats the current system of "anything goes," and "blind tradition rules." At the same time, it should give us a means for discarding misinterpretation, ignorance, and the bad science of the ancient world. It should cry out to the world that "...*the heavens declare the glory of God...*" and it should cause the world to cry back in return that "*the firmament showeth His handiwork.*" Important biblical verses like Psalms 19:1 have been left to atrophy under the assault of fundamentalism on science, and this should exist no more. It is time to recreate an era when theologians believed that science enhances the flowering of human understanding about God.

"Natural theology" provides a rich philosophical backdrop for the application of scriptural dynamism. We must remember, however, that "science" and "natural theology" are separate terms, with discrete and distinct connotations. On its own and in its most rigorous application, science is far from being a witness to God or a theological tool. It is instead only a rigorous method of getting at the truth about observable phenomena, and it is intended to deal only with what we can see, feel and touch. Its findings and conclusions are always based upon the weight of evidence at any one time (which can change). Many of us think of science not as the investigatory tool it is, but as a body of proven knowledge. Both slants can be correct. In either case, science is not automatically a doorway through which we can approach the divine. The Big Bang Theory, in a purely scientific context, only asserts that at a certain time, and under certain undefined circumstances, an explosion occurred which created our universe. While impressive evidence sustains the reality of that explosion and suggests that it led to our being, the Big Bang Theory (on its own) says nothing about *how and why* the Big Bang occurred, for there is no direct evidence of the hows and the whys. The theory starts only 10^{-46} seconds after the explosion began. It further incorporates no hypotheses about any universe that might have existed before the explosion. Hawking and other scientists, for example, employ a philosophical device called "Occam's Razor" to rationalize why it is scientifically preferable to simply "cut away" any consideration of events that might have occurred prior to the Big Bang. To them this excision *must* be made, because there is no *data* that can be obtained about what went on before our own universe existed. Only theology, or a speculative "composite" of scientific theory and theology, can speak to such topics. However, speculation is never an acceptable device for reaching sound scientific conclusions, and because of this the best scientists carefully avoid speculation as a matter of principle. This is all well and good if one is a practicing scientist. If we are examining the issue of the existence of God, pure science only leaves us hanging to a paradoxical branch of creation, above the paradoxical abyss of a universe that may someday be destroyed in flames. *All of us have the same desire—if our universe is going to someday bite* *the big one, we all want to know how, why **and when**!* Only theology, or "natural theology," can deal with such issues.

Biblical literalism, in separating us from the realities of science in a modern world, also separates us from half the truth. As shown in the foregoing chapters, it can cause us to disregard messages hidden in the scriptures, which can only be elucidated by a composite of science and scripture. Such is the case with Genesis 1:2 and its description of a "pre-creational universe," and its use of the phrases: "without form and void," and "darkness upon the face of the deep." Where does literalism speak of the association of black holes and creation?

It doesn't, but if we look deeply enough into the scriptures, and establish the proper context and meaning, we find that the Bible may have something very significant to say about this topic—and to me, at least, the implications are truly startling. In the English Language, the word "darkness" simply means the absence of light, and implies an inability to see. *In ancient Hebrew, however, there were **two distinct terms** for the English word "darkness."* The Hebrew word *"aphela"* was used to denote the absence of light, as in English, but the word *"**khoshekh**"* had a quite different twist—denoting a state of darkness that had its own unique *physical properties*. There is simply no equivalent concept in English. Complicating the situation is the fact that the distinction between *aphela* and *khoshekh* has largely disappeared in Modern Hebrew. *As one might expect, however, the original Genesis uses the word "khoshekh."* Does the scriptural use of "khoshekh" and its dead-ringer application to a black hole connect? A black hole would clearly possess "khoshekh," a state of darkness with its own unique, physical, properties! Assuming that a real God issued real Divine Revelation in the form of Genesis 1:1-3, using the word "khoshekh" in an effort to describe a primordial black hole, we happen upon a profound, and profoundly hidden message. The words of Genesis *are* **clearly telling us that the universe was in the form of a black hole prior to the moment of creation!**

But black holes are a product of 20th Century knowledge. The ancient Jews who gave us our earliest biblical interpretations and traditions would not have been even remotely able to conceive of such an object! They would have been forced by their ignorance into ultimately twisting "khoshekh" into "aphela"—into a tone and tenor, moreover, that they could grasp. And this is precisely what happened.

A real and omniscient God, however, would have known that the true meaning of the word "khoshekh" would have been indecipherable to those who received His Revelation. The reason why He went ahead and gave it can only lie in Calvinism—in God's desire to connect with humanity and to give evidence of his existence . in profound ways. As Calvin suggested, God gave words to the ancients that only formed a shadow of the appearance of things, but provided relatively clear directions for communion with God. Calvinism implicitly contains the notion that God instilled the scriptures with meaning that will inevitably spill forth in the fullness of time. At the same time, it tells us that there is something more important than our knowledge of the truths of the universe—i.e. God's desire to connect with us. Perhaps God intends to connect with us across the pages of eternity, past, present and future, demonstrating in profoundly effective and sometimes startling ways His being to all generations. As we can see in the "khoshekh" analogy, God seems to have designed His "Revelation" so that it can be traced to nothing but Him, and so that it will occasionally jump out and smack us in the face!

CHAPTER FOUR

THE SHARED LIGHT OF CREATION

Allegory: I am the spirit of your imagination. Travel with me. The time is before the universe was created. The darkness is thick, heavy, oppressive, stifling. All around me there is nothing, or at least there is nothing that I can see. I can sense movement, but I have no visual references to assure that I am really moving. It is cold, terribly, horrendously cold. I am all alone, as I have been for a great portion of eternity—a spirit floating, hovering, "existing" and little else in the great and infinite void. I cannot see because of the darkness, neither can I smell, nor touch, nor hear, nor laugh, nor speak. There is nothing here with me but my "being." My loneliness surpasses all hope of understanding! It has sapped my very essence and left me as cold as the endless and empty void that surrounds me.

A light! I see a light! Something is moving! Strangely, the mist that surrounds me is beginning to glow. I see something! Whatever it is, it is gloriously beautiful! This great light somehow gives me comfort! I feel myself accelerating, as if I am being pulled in its direction. I can clearly see an entity in the mist, now, moving about— moving across something dark and strange, something entirely without form and void. This wondrous entity somehow seems to radiate a great and glorious light which is being focused upon the shadow of this formless thing, this vast "black hole" in the fabric of the void.

Suddenly I feel vibrations! All around, there is an exploding stream of light and heat, and a rolling thunder of incredible magnitude!!! The void has turned white hot! The heat is incredible, far hotter than anything I could ever have imagined! Brilliant light is mushrooming outward now from the great black hole, inflating against and pushing back the blackness and desolate emptiness of the great eternal void! Could this finally be a new creation? All around me are fiery streams of matter, brighter and hotter than a million billion suns! I sense that soon there will be no more loneliness, no more perpetual darkness. Something wonderful has happened!

* * * *

"In the beginning God created the heavens and the earth. And the earth was without form and void; and darkness was upon the face of the deep. And the spirit of God moved upon the face of the waters. And God said: Let there be light, and there was light..." (Genesis 1:1-3)[26]

* * * *

The greatest of all composites of science and scripture is the "light correlation. *Light has a pivotal role IN BOTH Genesis and the Big Bang Theory, and this is the most obvious and compelling of all the parallels between scripture and science!* According to scripture, God brought the PHYSICAL universe into being AFTER the command "Let there be light..." According to the Big Bang Theory, the PHYSICAL universe came into being after the light of the Big Bang. **In both science and scripture, light brings forth creation.** As noted by physicist Hubert Reeves in "Atoms of Silence," a process well known to science explains why light is so integral to the creation process:

...there are in the cosmos, on the average, a billion photons of light for every atom. Why this number rather than another? It results in large part from events that occurred in the first microseconds (millionths of a second) of the universe...

During the first few seconds of the universe, matter and antimatter coexisted in the hot primal soup. They annihilated each other continuously to become light... (The creation *of matter and antimatter out of light and their annihilation back into light are not mere speculation. These events are of daily occurrence in nuclear physics laboratories.*)[27]

Reeves' quotation drives home an essential point—matter is formed from the collision of high energy light beams. However, the opposite also occurs—light (energy) is formed from colliding particles of matter. In a sense, then, the birth of our universe is reduced to the prototypical energy-matter transmutation explained in Einstein's "Special Theory of Relativity." It is just a bit astonishing that ancient Hebrew scriptures describing the events of creation, would settle, for no apparent reason, on light as the harbinger of creation. In some fanciful and patently untrue creation story written by some maniacal rabbi who just wanted to control people, why would it be necessary to have a deity say "Let there be light..."? Furthermore, the way light is expressed in Genesis (with the material universe immediately following the expression of light) hints of relativity. The problem is that special relativity could not possibly have been fathomed by human beings who lived 3,000 years ago, or even 300. So, from whence did this sequence of words in the creation story originate, and why?

The overwhelming significance of the light correlation, is that it sets forth facts that can be adequately explained *only* if we accept a premise that a higher and greater being participated in the writing of Genesis! So, while, on the one hand, there is clear historical evidence that portions of Genesis were written by men, the light correlation and descriptions of the pre-creational universe suggest that portions of Genesis *were written* under Divine Leadership.

Einstein's Special Theory of Relativity relates to several phenomena in our universe, but the part that really concerns us, at the moment in this book, is the portion embodied in the famous equation $E=MC^2$. The message delivered here is that under certain conditions, energy can become matter AND/OR matter can become energy. Light is simply a portion of the energy spectrum. In noting God's introduction of light *prior to* the formation of the physical universe, Genesis 1:3 brings scripture into direct correlation with the Big Bang Theory and special relativity. Reeves' quotation cuts to the essence, showing that in its first nanoseconds the universe was dominated by particles of energy (*virtual particles*), but that matter (*real particles*) springs from energy, and that this is precisely what happened in the Big Bang. The difference between Genesis and science is that in Genesis, GOD calls forth light—in science there is no explanation for the explosion and its released energy, since there is no overt data on how and why the explosion occurred—and what blew up. Yet, in both, light comes forth and creates! Scripture is therefore undeniably connected to the Big Bang, *and to special relativity.*

Those who favor the notion of an *accidental* creation, however, suggest that something entirely different happened, that matter somehow (mysteriously) underwent an exceedingly long and complex series of chemical and physical changes, and that such changes ultimately brought our universe into being. Their argument, which we will look at in far greater detail in the last few chapters, is completely predicated on the excision, via "Occam's Razor, of everything that happened before the moment of creation. There is no recognition of separate "alpha" and "omega" state universes. They could not accept the notion that gravity continues into the omega state universe as the great driving force of the great caissons of eternity, because they cannot accept anything that might have happened before the Big Bang. Furthermore, the notion of an accidental creation is attractive to many scientists because it frees them from the chains imposed by theologians.

Yet, science recognizes the creation as a very unique event. Astrophysicist George Greenstein notes (in a quotation appearing later) that the probability of the right mix of energy and matter occurring accidentally so as to unleash a process of creation *is so small as to be infinite*, and that creation must therefore be regarded as a supreme act of "perfection."[28] Hawking's *Brief History of Time* contains a similar assertion. Sir Fred Hoyle, one of the revisers and founders of the modern Steady State Theory, has likened the probability of an accidental creation to the probability of a tornado careening through a junkyard and accidentally assembling a Boeing 747. But in a review of literature, support for a "Divine Creation," among noted scientists, always comes up missing.

I believe that "my interpretation" of the first three verses of Genesis has been corroborated by significant findings such as the "hierarchy of black holes," which suggest how a prior universe might ultimately have been crunched into oblivion, and then recreated. I believe that there is no way to account for the Big Bang, except via the awesome power of God. I believe that God somehow connected with an imponderable black hole in the moments before the creation (note the phrase: …"and God moved upon the face of the waters"), and did His thing, and the result is you sitting there today, reading my words. Scripture plainly describes God's movements in the pre-creational environment, and this movement and activity may explain what happened. It isn't that it should explain what happened precisely, but that it links God to the creation, in no uncertain terms. Could there have been a release of pure, unadulterated, divine energy into the black hole, which caused the explosion? Obviously, such speculation is *far* beyond the realm of science, but it is well within the realm of theology (though literalists have not been adept enough to notice it). Hawking's process for exploding a black hole presupposes the availability of infalling matter, the destruction of which provides the necessary virtual particles that ultimately destroy the black hole. For a black hole in our existing, alpha-state universe, such matter would be readily available, but in the case of a black hole in an omega-state universe, all matter should (theoretically) already be encapsulated within the black hole. Therefore, there would be nothing available to issue virtual particles into the black hole. A universe *completely* encapsulated in a black hole could not come out and experience a recreation. There is simply no way around this problem. For an omega-state universe to come out of its collapsed state, there would have to be an outside source of energy, and that source would have to be virtually infinite. Guess who's existence is justified by all of this!

Then along comes the "light correlation," which intimately ties science to scripture, and everything to God, and the word "khoshekh" describing a darkness with substance in the pre-creational universe! The scene set by Genesis, in my opinion, is that of The Divine transforming a quasi-*infinite* material *mass* into a quasi-infinite mass of energy via His own ***infinite power***! Western civilization has come to view God in terms that are very personable. God has been painted into our imagination as an old man with long, white hair and a long, flowing white beard. Because Genesis suggests that we were created in His image, it has become acceptable to think in terms of a God Who is a person. To Christians, this idea seems to have been reinforced by Christ, the very human and finite, yet Divine Son of God. However, a being limited to a defined body (or defined area) is implicitly limited in His access to energy. The only way to be unlimited in energy and power is to be unlimited in dimensional expanse. This suggests that the real deity is necessarily "pantheistic," in the sense that He *is* everywhere and **is** simultaneously at one with the universe. At the same time, this pantheism should not necessarily preclude Him from having a discrete intellect and persona and assuming a recognizable form. However, any true physical or material being would be unable to survive the oscillation of the universe, and would be destroyed either in the "Big Crunch" or the "Big Bang." So, scientific reasoning—like the Bible, itself—tells us that God cannot be a physical being.

A "***virtual being***," on the other hand, would be able to survive such an event. (In Chapters Eight and Nine we will explore the idea of a "virtual being" more closely). A virtual being might also be quite capable of being "pantheistic." The Bible implicitly suggests that God is all around us, and that theme is particularly prevalent in the Book of Psalms. The same theme is echoed in the Gospel of Thomas (Verse 77), where Jesus says: "I am the all... Split wood; I am there. Lift up a stone, and you will find me there." This statement turns out to be one of the primary reasons why the Gospel of Thomas has not been accepted as one of the canonical gospels. But there are many theologians who believe that Thomas deserves a higher status. If Jesus is truly one with God (as Christians contend), then it is God Who tells us in the Gospel of Thomas that He is physically everywhere and conterminous with the substance of this universe. We certainly know that the concept of a Ptolemaic deity is incorrect, and this, unfortunately, is still the notion of God and the model of the universe that is favored by many fundamentalists. If the foregoing words were truly spoken by Jesus, and if Jesus is truly at one with God, as the concept of the Holy Trinity suggests, His description of Himself as a pantheistic entity conterminous with the substance of the universe in the Gospel of Thomas is indeed fascinating, at the very least.

I suspect that any theologian would contend that a prayer uttered by an astronaut standing on the surface of Mars would be just as readily heard by God as one uttered by a person standing in his front yard on Earth. I suspect that any theologian would also tell us that if both such prayers were uttered simultaneously, both would be simultaneously heard by God. Our traditional way of looking at God, however, doesn't address the riddle of how this is possible.

In traditional Judaism, Christianity and Islam, the universe is distinctly separate from God, or Allah, but this separation can only be rationalized via a Ptolemaic model of the universe—and that has been shown to be patently incorrect. Theologians have traditionally held that God could not possibly be "at one" with us, because in doing so He would become a participant in our sins—and God fundamentally cannot look upon sin. At the same time, every theologian would contend that God knows about each sin that we commit at the precise moment in which we commit it. Such views just don't synchronize. God has to have a way of receiving information—but how? Isn't this typical of traditional theology—strike it off as a mystery and then tell everyone not to worry about it because it's God's business and not ours! Based as it is upon past knowledge and ancient traditions, theology has rendered God innately paradoxical, and traditional theologians have allowed themselves to become content to shrug their shoulders and exclaim: "God is a mystery," or to exclaim that "it isn't intended for us to know such things—that one should just have faith!" Faith is wonderful, but in a modern world where believers are continually barraged by opposing, atheistic ideas and evidence that contradicts the basis of ancient theology, reason and understanding can also be a key to greater faith. Theologians have simply ignored the powerful, potential contributions of science and the intellectual demands of the 21st Century. Being focused on the past, and fearful of ideas implicit in modern science, such as Darwinism, they have sometimes made God into something that He truly isn't.

In Hinduism, the universe is indistinct from Brahman (the supreme deity), and is, in fact, considered to be a manifestation of Brahman. The Mundaka Upanishad (Hindu holy book) likens the growing of plants from the soil and hair from the body to the process by which the universe came forth from Brahman. According to this notion, the supreme deity spans and engulfs the entire universe and all that is within it. The problem with this view (from the perspective of Jews, Christians and Moslems) is that Brahman doesn't seem to possess a well-defined persona and will. If there is a divinely-orchestrated purpose for man, and for the remainder of the universe, it is ambiguous at best in Hinduism. The traditional Judeo-Christian notion of God as a distinct manlike persona may be correct in expressing the notion of a God Who possesses an intellect and will, which is singular and definable, but otherwise in defining how God could be omniscient, omnipresent and omnipotent, it strikes out and it seems farther from the truth than the Hindu version which spreads deity into all portions of the universe.

Certainly, the Ptolemaic notion of a distinct supernatural being looking down upon us through an enclosed sphere, controlling every facet of our existence in a tiny, astrodome-style, earth-centered universe, is one that is incorrect. Yet, this sort of image of God is very deeply ingrained in almost everything that we do. When we pray to "God above...," when we ask Him to show mercy on sinners "here below...," when we think of a heaven above the clouds—in all of these circumstances we are unconsciously conjuring up the Ptolemaic Model of a flat Earth and a geocentric universe of enclosed spheres, a model that has been thoroughly discredited. Such antiquated belief systems create the wrong image of God! Tradition is lovely and quaint, and it provides security, but when it is obviously incorrect, it is not automatically our friend! So, where is God? The *God Theory* will suggest that He is right here, all around us, and within us.

So Who and What is God? In the final chapters we will examine this topic in greater depth. For the moment, it is sufficient to conclude that *God is an intelligent, omnipotent, unbounded, "virtual" or "energy-being," Who is perhaps more closely related to the "forces of nature" than to real matter*. The notion of God as a virtual being is not counter to the Bible, the Torah, or the Koran! In the Bible, for example, God is typically described as a spiritual being of overwhelming radiance, as one of extreme brilliance, having a fiery appearance, or as being surrounded by a field of glowing energy (a halo), etc. No physical being could possess such characteristics. At the Red Sea, God took the form of a "Pillar of Fire" and blocked the advance of Pharaoh's chariots. Before that, He appeared to Moses as a "burning bush." To Ezekiel, He appeared as the image of a radiant man engulfed in a great cloud of raging fire. The scriptures consistently tell us that no one could look upon God and survive. In Christian, Hebrew and Islamic traditions, barriers to physical interaction between God and man stem from the fact that God is righteous and man is lowly and sinful. Yet, such barriers could also stem from God's basic nature as a being of vast and overwhelming energy. Is this, in fact, why no one in the Bible was able to look upon God and survive? Is this why, today, that no one can look unshielded into the heart of a nuclear reactor and survive?

The God Who emerges from this analysis has no need to create by magic. He is One Who creates by the intelligent and purposeful manipulation of matter and energy, Whose existence is sustained in the theories of relativity and quantum mechanics, and Who is innately at one with the universe. The composite of science and scripture suggests that He simply extended His Being across the face of a colossal black hole (paraphrasing Genesis), focused His enormous power upon the pre-creational universe dominated as it was by a massive black hole, and then caused a sudden, massive hemorrhage of its "mass." This, of course, was followed by a sudden burst of atomic movement, and the "Big Bang." The rest is history.

CHAPTER FIVE

FOUNDATIONS OF BEING

As we have seen in the foregoing chapter, science and scripture pointedly concur on the importance of light in creation, forming a *profound composite* which suggests that a single event, the Big Bang, stacked the cards of creation so as to unfold the current scheme of things. Scriptural creation begins with the creation of light. Scientific creation begins with the Big Bang. The foundations of our being are linked to God by the Big Bang and gravity. Gravity caused our galaxy to condense, and our solar system and planet to accrete into being. It then engendered critical geological processes which led to the development of a living ecosystem. In this and the following chapter we shall examine our ties to God and see how/why our being is inevitably rooted in the Big Bang. We shall also continue to examine the overall importance of gravity—the first great force of nature that was released in the grand explosion.

At the precise moment of the Big Bang, there was nothing in the universe but energy. The tiniest fraction of a nanosecond afterwards, matter appeared. The universe was thus driven from a state of high disorder, during the explosion, to a state of increasing stability and equilibria in the moments, millennia and eons afterward. This trend from disorder to increasing order has continued ever since. It is as if the universe has a natural "anti-entropy," which moves it from rare, brief states of utter chaos, like the "Big Bang" toward extended phases of increasing balance and quiescence. Yet, it appears that this trend can be reversed. Certainly, there was greater order in the pre-explosive phase universe than during and immediately after the explosion. It is now becoming clear that since the time of the Big Bang, gravity (which we can also refer to as "anti-entropy") has driven our universe inexorably toward an omega phase universe. Were this not the case, the existing universe would have no "black holes." A steady progression toward the omega phase must therefore be recognized as a general trend of our universe—a trend with far-reaching implications for everything. We see it in the tendency of atoms to bond into molecular compounds to achieve neutrality, and in the tendency, over time, for both atoms and compounds to become increasingly complex. Entropy has dominated our universe on a grand scale because of the dispersal of matter engendered by the Big Bang, but this is not the case when we move to the galactical level. As great blobs of matter dispersed from the Big Bang, they progressively condensed into smaller and smaller units. So, even as the entropy of the universe was increasing due to the outspreading of the galaxies, the forces of anti-entropy were drawing together matter around great galactical lumps. ***Of all the effects of anti-entropy, the most profound is EVOLUTION. Evolution is a prevailing trend and progression of our universe linked intimately to the force of gravity. The evolution of matter and the physical universe has been the most visible trend of our universe since the beginning of time***. At first, the universe contained only energy in the form of a hot fireball, then particles emerged from the collision of high-energy light beams, then as the fireball cooled, particles differentiated into protons, electrons and neutrons. Later, these cooled and gravitationally coalesced into the first hydrogen atoms. In time, simple elements such as hydrogen and helium were cycled through new stellar furnaces and the outputs of these processes produced slightly complex elements such as sodium and potassium. Further cycling through stellar furnaces then resulted in aluminum, silicon, calcium, magnesium, carbon, and iron, etc. With each successive generation of stars, the universe evolved an increasingly complex chemistry. A few billion years after the Big Bang, the continuation of this process resulted in the appearance of organic molecules, and a few billion years later, an exceedingly complex organic molecule somehow came into being that was able to cross the boundary between the living and nonliving, and thereafter it replicated itself. This gave rise to *living* compounds, and perpetuated a cycle that we now call life. And so it is that life is just another output of the prevailing trend of the universe since the Big Bang. Life, like chemistry, is a product of a universe perpetually struggling to attain order and balance. Complexity became an inevitable result of the natural progression of things.

Fundamentalist and conservative theologians have long objected to this view of the universe, arguing that it ultimately restricts God from the miraculous. They suggest that if natural forces and trends achieved creation, God becomes little more than a detached observer. The notion of a unique and separate creation for everything is more majestic, according to their point of view, and more in line with scriptural expression. Great miracles and unique acts of God are a biblical mainstay. These include the plagues of Egypt and the parting of the Red Sea, Joshua collapsing the walls of Jericho, Elijah calling fire down from heaven, Jesus healing the sick and raising the dead. All of these things occurred under Divine authority, and God directly performed many other miracles, Himself—not the least of which was the creation.

The "irreconcilers" among both scientists and theologians are the ones who have chiefly carried on the debate about miracles. The moderates, however, are able to see that "evolution" is itself a miracle—and perhaps the greatest of miracles—because it is the result of a Great God stacking the cards of creation with such sublime precision at the moment of creation that nature would end up producing His pre-defined goals—on a truly grand scale. Such a thing, to me, is far more miraculous than the notion of a deity creating us individually.

The notion of "*Theistic Evolution*" suggests that God pre-ordained the universe to be the way it is via the mix of energy and matter in the fires of the Big Bang. Evolution is simply the process by which God achieved creation. It is as if He planted the seeds of our current universe in the fires of the Big Bang, and any control over them individually was primarily exercised at a grand scale. The essential point is that God achieved creation by *process*, not *magic*. Unlike creationism, theistic evolution *sweeps away the notion of magical commands followed by the materialization of the Earth, a fish, a tree, etc. What a creationist views as a miracle, the theistic evolutionist views as a natural Act of an Omnipotent Being Who exercises vast control over the forces of nature—naturally. If one wants to continue to use the term "miracle"—fine, but the evidence suggests that "miracles" are only matters of Divine Choice exercised via the manipulation of nature to achieve a Divine goal. Words like supernatural and miraculous only stem from our basic inability to understand the fundamental nature and being of God, the way He constructed our universe, and the control He has over it. At God's level what we would call "miracles," are just part of the natural order of things!*

Scriptural dynamism contains elements of the "deism" that surfaced during the so-called "Age of Reason" (the latter 18th and early 19th centuries). This was an era that produced a number of well-known "deists," some of whom occupied center stage during the American Revolution. The most prominent was Thomas Jefferson. Jefferson believed that the orderly movements of the heavenly bodies, the structure of the Earth, and even life, itself, reflected a grand design, and the existence of a Grand Designer. Benjamin Franklin was another prominent deist who had very similar views, including a belief that the personality, the *"being"* of a person, somehow survived eternity. Both Jefferson and Franklin equated, "freedom of religion" to "freedom *from* religion," as was the mode among *all* deists. The era's most eloquent "deist," was Thomas Paine. Like Jefferson, Paine believed that the order and harmony reflected in the movements of the heavenly bodies reflected a grand design (and he wrote eloquently about this in his "Age of Reason"). But Paine's reasoning added another important and (by now) familiar twist to the philosophy of the deists—the notion that anything introduced as the "Word of God" *must give evidence of being what it is called—that it must correlate to the grand design that is readily observed in nature. Paine insisted that a true deity would ensure consistency between nature and scripture, and that a true theology must reflect that same harmony and consistency.* To Paine and other deists, the pathway to God led inevitably through rationalism and reason. Rationalism was not a tool used by deists such as Paine for striking down the greatness of God, as many fundamentalists have asserted (then and now). Instead, it was simply a measuring device designed to gauge the accuracy of religious teachings! The notion of a Grand Design reflected in Creation was among the strongest tenets of deism and early rationalism, and this inevitably led to belief in an innate harmony between nature and scripture. It was a goal of Paine and other deists of his day to have this message reflected in all human teachings.

However, Paine and most other deists often vehemently opposed organized religion. They argued that the "organized," or "revealed," religions were uniformly *irrational* and *inconsistent*—that on the one hand, the *Calvinists* condemned all but a few redeemed to burn in hell for an eternity, while on the other hand the *Universalists* dropped everyone off at heaven's gate, regardless of the horror and multitude of their sins. Paine and Franklin rejected all revealed religions as a mockery of the grand design and implicit harmony between nature and scripture—which they believed to be a critical facet of creation. The calling card and password of all deists was a simple and direct belief in a Creator, a grand design, and a rationalistic harmony between science and scripture. Mahatma Ghandi can be seen as a modern era deist and rationalist. Ghandi, as we have noted previously, found inconsistencies among the great religions of the world, in much the same manner as Paine, Jefferson and Franklin, and he added an important suggestion that all revealed religions suffer from a problem called "double distillation," in which divine revelation is inexorably subverted by human cultural baggage and tradition.

The notions of "order" and "grand design" reflected in deism and rationalism are obviously rooted in earlier ideas. To an extent, they can be thought of as throwbacks to "geocentrism," to the notion of a universe ordered into discrete spheres, and into a gradation of perfection. This notion of "order" ultimately made its way through deism into natural theology and modern naturalism. But the naturalists, after Darwin, moved sharply in the direction of agnosticism, and by the 20th Century they had begun to refute the notion of "order" and tout the notion of "randomness," as the primary guiding principle of evolution. However, the notion of "order" as a prerequisite for a divine creation is simply an expression of a longstanding trend in thought. There is no fundamentally essential reason why God would have had to have given us a universe that is perfectly orderly in every respect.

Steeped in tradition and without benefit of modern scientific knowledge, our forebears "distilled" many different notions about God and Creation into the Christian faith, and many of those have only limited scriptural basis. The notion of order is one example. Another is the belief in a somewhat mystical creation in which God simply spoke everything into existence. To many, it was as if God's only creation tools were the spoken word, or thought, and Creation was thus treated as a magical event in which God simply "POOFED" the universe and all lifeforms into being in six successive phases, spanning six 24-hour days! This view of creation precluded God from stepping back and letting evolution do its thing after He had initiated the various phases. The scriptures, however, do not preclude this if one translates the term day as a "sphere of time."

Christian tradition further attempts to discourage lay and scientific efforts to explain the creation via known scientific processes. This can be traced to the Age of Reason, when the clergy felt threatened by scientific progress and deemed such efforts heretical and sinful. Yet, there is absolutely no reason why Christians should favor mysticism over reason, or why theologians should discourage efforts to explain the creation. Explaining God and creation will not detract from His omniscience, omnipotence, and omnipresence. There is no innate reason why process is sinful, and why God would not want to create via "process." To say that everything was done mystically only imposes our limitations upon God. Yet, clerical traditions suggest that anything that smacks of PROCESS somehow "constrains" or encumbers God's. What kind of crazy logic is this?

We remain stuck in an antiquated theology that is in major need of renovation. There is no reason why a God Who is *in control of everything*, and Who is at one with everything, would fundamentally avoid the use of processes that He innately controls. We live in the 21st Century, and not the 16th. Our 16th Century forefathers had a reasonable excuse for their biblical misinterpretation—they were scientifically ignorant. Theirs was a tiny, astrodome-type universe centered on a flat Earth, surrounded by liquid, heavenly waters—which, in turn, was ringed by outlying spheres, the outermost being heaven, itself. They explained God by asserting that He was supernatural and beyond human understanding, and they used their heritage of superstitious incantation and mystical conjuring to interpret the Genesis Account of Creation. Doctrine was subsequently cast in blood and iron, and enforced by theological terrorism.

Today, science is increasingly imposing checks and balances upon this mystical theological heritage. This has angered fundamentalists, who prefer the free exercise of literalism and 16th Century science. However, even in the 16th Century theologians such as John Calvin had enough sense to realize that literalism was not an adequate tool for nailing down and/or uncovering the precise meaning of scripture. Calvin knew that literalism always leaves much to the imagination, and that science was, in fact, the best tool for uncovering real scriptural meaning. The problem with literalism is that it usually leaves gaping holes that very often *must* be filled with something just to achieve adequate communication. As a good example of this—one of my geology students once brought up the issue of human age: "before Noah," she said, "people often lived 700 to 900 years, but today they only live about one tenth that long. The people in her church had explained away that discrepancy by noting that before Noah, the overlying "heavenly waters" filtered out the ultra violet rays of the sun, and this allowed them to live longer…"! She later described herself as an atheist. Such is the case with creationism and what it does for people. The Bible says nothing about the UV-flux, which is a concern that arose in the 20th Century, but here it is influencing a wild new fundamentalist creationism. The fact of the matter is that all types of half-baked, non-scientific theories are now being offered by fundamentalist theologians to explain the creation events, shore up literalism, and discredit science. Whatever their present devotion to this cause, history will ultimately pronounce them to be in error, and time will prove that the best biblical gap-fillers are history, archaeology and science—not human imagination.

How can we accurately use science to fill in the scriptural gaps? Obviously, this entire book attempts to answer that question. No biblical scriptures leap forth from the creation story to describe the formation of the Great Attractor, Andromeda, the Milky Way Galaxy, our solar system, or the Planet Saturn with its magnificent rings. There is no mention of Sirius, Betelgeuse, Alpha Centauri, Mars, or the moons of Jupiter—*it is only because of science that we know of the existence of such heavenly bodies. E*ither science, human imagination or popular mythology will **always** color our interpretations of Genesis! So, which one is it?

Evidence suggests that Mesopotamian mythology and bad science colored the theology of the Hebrew Priests of Babylon, and, in turn, was distilled into the doctrines of the early Christian church. In our generation, we cannot accept such an erroneous and half-baked theological heritage. Mushrooming scientific knowledge will quickly make it seem that all Judeo-Christian theologians are liars unless they begin to accept and embrace the facts of science. The only option is rejection of theological traditionalism and development of a more accurate, futuristic theology. The question is not whether this will occur, in my opinion, but when, and whether the resulting theology will resemble the current. The Genesis creation story can only be completed by science, for only in science are there reasonably accurate answers about the mysteries of the universe, the nature of eternity, and the existence of God.

As I began to develop *The God Theory*, it became very clear to me that the key to an understanding of the nature of God is a comprehension of the nature of gravity. In the next few chapters I will show that the impact of gravity as a creative force is clearly and completely evident in every phase of creation! This is not unlike the creative "Hand of God." The original cosmic gascloud that was formed after the Big Bang gravitationally collapsed into protogalaxies to form the basic outlines of our existing universe. As atoms continued to form, energy from the Big Bang not tied up in sub-atomic movements slowly dissipated to space. All the while, space continued to darken. Soon, the universe was divided into glowing embers of Creation and a perpetual background of darkness:

> In the early universe space was brilliantly illuminated. As time passed, the fabric of space continued to expand, the radiation cooled and, in ordinary visible light, for the first time space became dark, as it is today.[29]

Genesis contains similar language:

Verse Four:

> ...and God divided the light from the darkness.

Verse Six:

> Then God said, "Let there be a firmament in the midst of the waters, and let it *divide* the waters from the waters."[30]

Where Genesis provides only a phrase or sentence, science typically adds a book, or perhaps an entire library. Science tells us that as darkness was being divided from light, atoms were differentiating and clumping together. At the same time, immensely hot clouds of gas left over from the fires of creation were contracting, gravitationally, to form the framework of the galaxies. Space and matter separated. No hardshell firmament appeared, and the universe did not become a tiny, domed stadium, as the ancients believed. Instead, lines of separation formed between the glowing gases of the primordial galaxies and the emptiness of space. Within these protogalaxies, continuing gravitational accretion ultimately awakened the first great suns. These burned for only a few hundred million years and then died an explosive death. In their death throes, however, they spewed out new and heavier elements and bequeathed the universe a richer substance. New elements were then cycled into a new generation of stars. Successive generations of stars were then born, each adding new elements to the universe in the same manner.[31] At some point in time, complex compounds and amino acids came into being—the organic precursors of life.

Four to eight billion years after the Big Bang, the Milky Way Galaxy had filled itself with hot, young stars. The galaxy also contained vast, thick clouds of interstellar gas and dust that continued to collapse gravitationally, and produce new stars. At some point in time, a star adjacent to a certain relatively dense cloud of gas and dust exploded, seeding that cloud with stellar remnants, new elements, and enough new mass to accelerate a significant gravitational collapse. Vast amounts of matter slowly and ponderously spiraled inward toward the center of an increasingly dense cloud. Perhaps a billion years passed as hot, swirling starstuff accreted into a growing proto-sun. Farther out from the center of the cloud, thousands of tiny planetesimals would slowly coalesce into proto-planets. The process was exceedingly slow and arduous. Gravitational collapse increased the opportunity for subatomic collision, and made the densest accumulations of matter increasingly hot. Heat, of course, only accelerated subatomic motion, which again increased the opportunity of subatomic collision. More and more collisions created a vicious cycle. Angular momentum was thus born from surplus catch-22 thermodynamic energy, the result being a swirling new proto-stellar system that gradually flattened itself out into a pinwheel spinning around the axis of an increasingly hot and dense proto-sun.

Long after the start of this process, when most of the matter had been gravitationally scooped up either by the proto-sun or proto-planets, space began to clear of its perpetual haze. The developing new star and its offspring were now illuminated as hot, dense, gaseous circles against the blackness of the void. Space in the vicinity of these circles was rapidly cooling, while the circles themselves were increasing in temperature. As a result, outside surfaces cooled slightly, and cooling put a damper on sub-atomic motion. This allowed the Pauli Exclusion Principle to work the proto-sun and proto-planets into an even denser and more compact arrangement. The Earth and its spinning sisters were now so dense, internally, that exotic new chemical phases began to form. Deep inside the planets, liquid and then solid iron began to condense. The new planets entered their final period of gestation. At this stage of creation, all the planets resembled the outer gas giants of today (i.e. Jupiter, Saturn, Uranus or Neptune), and the proto-sun had become a roaring inferno—its internal heat approaching critical mass. As it actually attained critical mass, it dispatched a stream of high-velocity subatomic particles which astrophysicists have called the *"T-Tauri Wind."* The birth of this particle stream was soon thereafter augmented by the blasts of the sun's great new fusion furnaces. A massive shock wave followed, rushed outward and blew away the great gaseous atmospheric envelopes of the inner planets.

Naked against the hot new sun and the mighty T-Tauri wind lay the Earth's steaming hot surface, visible for the first time ever, foreboding and partially molten. However, over ensuing millennia, cooling would gradually harden and stabilize the surface, encapsulating an unstable mass of interstellar volatiles in the process that would later have a profound impact.

Then, about 4.6 billion years ago, the mantle crystallized solid *olivine*, marking the planet's official birth as a solid, stable entity. Though the mantle and crust had largely solidified, many portions of the outer Earth remained hot and pliable until the mid-Archean, about 3.5 billion years ago (BYA). Between 4.6 and 3.5 BYA, portions of the crust were often given to great fits of volcanism and destruction. Huge portions would melt, cool, form plateau basalts, heat and then recycle. Gradual cooling, of course, brought increasing stability. As the crust increasingly solidified, however, it was unable to indefinitely contain the volatiles that had been trapped inside during the accretionary phase. As noted by Hubert Reeves in *Atoms of Silence*, a period of outgassing was inevitable:

> At their birth, planets are balls of incandescent lava...
> Under the formidable meteoritic avalanche that gave it
> birth, our planet seems to have remained in a liquid
> state for many millions of years... As our planet in the
> process of formation sweeps through space in its early
> orbit, it gathers up all the stones and dust that cross its
> path. This dust—rocky nuclei surrounded by layers of
> ice—is devoured by the red incandescent ball... What
> becomes of these specks in the molten mass? They first
> evaporate and then dissolve in the interior of the Earth...
> Liquid rock can incorporate large quantities of gaseous
> material, but solid rock cannot. When the first terrestrial
> crust is formed, openings appear, like volcanic rents.
> In mighty geysers, masses of gas escape to the surface...
> The planet becomes clothed in a vast, dense
> atmosphere... Water begins to condense. It rains as it
> will never rain again. It rains entire oceans.[32]

Thus, outgassing provided for an atmosphere and the first
primitive accumulations of water on the surface. Modern evidence
also suggests that outgassing may have been richly supplemented by
barrages of asteroids and comets that contained a significant amount
of H_2O, and perhaps even the seeds of life. During the next billion
years or so, the combined output/input of volatiles led to the formation
of shallow oceans across much of the planet's inhospitable surface.
*Remarkably, the Yahwist Account of Creation in Genesis 2:4-6 seems
to describe this same sort of outgassing process:*

> 4 These are the generations of the heavens and of the
> earth when they were created, in the DAY THAT THE
> LORD GOD MADE THE EARTH AND THE
> HEAVENS.
> 5 And every plant of the field BEFORE IT WAS IN
> THE EARTH, and every herb of the field BEFORE IT
> GREW: for the Lord God had not caused it to rain upon

the earth, AND THERE WAS NOT YET A MAN TO
TILL THE GROUND.
**6 BUT THERE WENT UP A MIST FROM THE
EARTH, AND WATERED THE WHOLE FACE OF
THE GROUND.**[33]

Interpreted in the light of science, the foregoing passage suggests
that before the existence of man, plant or any other living creature, a
mist escaped from fissures in the Earth's crust, rose up into the
atmosphere, experienced adiabatic cooling (as all rising moisture
does), condensed and rained down upon the surface. The biblical
account of this event is not only similar to Reeves' description, it
also concurs with prominent geological theories on the origin of the
Earth's atmosphere and oceans.

Even as the Earth's crust became cool, brittle and stable, hot
convection currents deep within the mantle continued to cause
upwelling of magma. Hot magma against cold crust created
instability, folding, fracturing, and rifting of the crust. Under constant
pressure from internal forces, massive portions of the crust ultimately
cracked and separated into distinct tectonic plates. Continued rapid
convection within the mantle then kept these plates moving and
interacting. When plates that were relatively light in density collided
the result was typically reverse faulting, mountain building, and
intrusive granitic magmatism. When plates rifted apart, the result
was typically normal faulting, formation of distinctive valleys, and
outpouring of basaltic magmas. Modern earthforming processes
began to take hold and leave their imprint upon the Earth's surface.
Throughout the Archean, volcanoes spewed nutrients, islands
coalesced into continents, shallow seas deepened, and mountains
rose and created barriers to the movement of moisture inland. The
first inland deserts were born and the first humid coastal plains. At
this stage in the Earth's history, however, true ocean basins did not
yet exist. Though primitive lifeforms might reside in shallow Archean
pools, a truly modern ecosystem would require real oceans and not
primitive, shallow "epeiric" seas. Genesis, in fact, seems to describe

a vital transformation in the surface of our primitive world that led to formation of discrete oceanic and continental assemblages:

> 9 Then God said, "Let the waters under the heavens be gathered together into ONE PLACE, and let the dry land appear; and it was so.[34]

The birth of a discrete world-ocean, a "panthallasa" (or all-seas) simultaneously gave rise to a discrete supercontinent, the first "pangaea" (or all-lands), and it is the latter that we have a distinct geologic record of. Science tells us that a "supercontinent" probably appeared near the start of the Proterozoic Eon. The term "Proterozoic" describes the third great "eon" of geologic time. Many geologists divide the timescale for the universe into *four great eons*: **(1)** the "*Catarchean*," which began with the Big Bang and ended with the crystallization of the Earth's mantle about 4.6 BYA; **(2)** the "*Archean*," which began with the crystallization of the mantle, produced the first continents, oceans, and lifeforms, and ended with the appearance of complex unicellular organisms called "green algae" about 2.5 BYA; **(3)** the "*Proterozoic*," which began as colonies of eukaryotic micro-organisms—the true antecedents of complex modern lifeforms—began to fill the oceans; it included prominent events such as the oxygenation of the atmosphere and the appearance of the first "metazoan" multicellular lifeforms; and **(4)** the modern "*Phanerozoic*," which is distinguished by the radiation and proliferation of complex lifeforms and the appearance of major elements of our modern ecosystem.

The first lifeforms—primitive archaebacteria and prokaryotic (anucleated) anaerobic bacteria—appeared early in the Archean, but very little evolutionary progress was made until much later. The "Proterozoic" is clearly distinguished from the Archean by the appearance in the fossil record of relatively advanced algae and protozoans. It is significant that such creatures appeared at or about the time of appearance of the "Early Proterozoic Supercontinent" ("EPS" for short).

Existence of the EPS is inferred by: (1) the so-called "Hudsonian Orogeny" (mountain-building episode) which produced worldwide orogenic (mountain) belts and patterns of continental uplifting, and (2) studies of global "paleomagnetism," which analyzes very old, undisturbed, magnetized rock formations in an effort to establish the past location of continents in relation to the poles. Mountain-building almost always results from compressive stresses caused by colliding continental plates. An orogenic *"belt"* suggests major continental accretion and collision across a wide portion of the Earth's surface. A truly major continental accretion is indicated at 2.5 billion years ago because orogenic belts of that age are found on all continents. Paleomagnetic evidence also backs an interpretation that every sizable landmass on Earth was incorporated into a supercontinental assemblage. In other words, evidence that all of the continents came together 2.5 billion years ago is significant. We have the two main indicators—orogenic belts and paleomagnetic indicators. Secondary evidence also supplements this conclusion—such as *basaltic* magmatism and rifting scars showing supercontinental breakup a few tens of millions of years later. Very old plateau basalts along the periphery of some of the Hudsonian orogenic belts shows distinct rifting-associated volcanism, a hallmark of continental breakup.

Because of the Early Proterozoic Supercontinent, we know that: "By approximately 2,500 million years ago the present volumes and areas of continents had been welded together" (King).[35] We also know that as the landforms came together, changes in the distribution of nutrients occurred along the continental margins. This may have stressed *prokaryotic organisms* (anucleated bacteria) in the peripheral oceans. As a result, unicellular eukaryotic (nucleated) lifeforms seem to have arisen opportunistically to fill new niches. Eukaryotes would ultimately form the basis of all complex lifeforms. Recent DNA studies have shown similarities between prokaryotes and the tiny "organelles" within eukaryotic cells, suggesting that the first eukaryotic cells may, in fact, have arisen from symbiotic amalgamation of prokaryotes.

Because the older and more primitive prokaryotes were

anucleated, and without a concentration of DNA in an enclosed nucleus, they were incapable of SEXUAL reproduction. New prokaryotes entered the world through "binary fission" in which one cell simply split itself into two. Prokaryotic offspring were thus *perfect clones* of their parents. Changes from one generation to the next occurred only as a result of genetic damage or mutation. Major evolutionary change occurred very, very slowly. Eukaryotic cells, by contrast, possessed well-developed nuclei, swapped genetic code during sexual reproduction, and exhibited considerable genetic variation from one generation to the next. Those best-suited for a particular environment survived and passed on their genetic code to new generations. Eukaryotic variation thus allowed rapid adaptation to new environmental niches and a veritable explosion of eukaryotic forms.

The great significance of the Early Proterozoic supercontinental accretion is that it created environmental conditions that allowed rapid ascension and radiation of eukaryotes. In so doing, it laid an essential foundation for the advent of higher lifeforms on Earth, including human beings. All of the higher lifeforms of our planet are descendants of simple unicellular eukaryotes.

Because the rise of eukaryotic organisms was triggered by geological events (i.e. the formation of the Early Proterozoic Supercontinent), it is increasingly clear that life on Earth is very intimately associated with the Earth's dynamic geological system— which is an inevitable result of the emergence of the force of gravity from the fires of the Big Bang. Gravity caused the formation and evolution of galaxies, the birth of our solar system, and ultimately the accretion of an Earth big enough and hot enough (internally) to drive a system of "plate tectonics." Plate tectonics would then serve as a great driving force for biological evolution. In an exceedingly important sense, then, our planet and ecosystem is a product of the Big Bang and the force of gravity.

Because of gravity, our world attained enough size and mass to engender significant internal heat, which, in turn, ultimately caused the onset of a worldwide system of plate tectonics. This led to what is popularly known as continental drift, which facilitated the appearance of eukaryotes as the biological basis for all higher lifeforms, and which has been a major driving force behind long-term biological change. Gravity as the first force of nature that appeared after the Big Bang, is intimately linked to the Big Bang, which is, in turn, intimately linked to the Divine Words: "Let there be light," and to the great caissons of eternity that forever drive the universe between the *alpha* and the *omega*. *We are, therefore, inescapably linked to God by observable forces of nature, the most prominent of which is gravity*. No scientist would dispute the existence of these forces and processes, but many, as we will see in the ensuing chapters, would dispute their linkage to God.

CHAPTER SIX

LIFE

The purpose of this chapter is to show how life fits into the foregoing scheme of physical evolution. The biological foundations of our own being were built upon the "eukaryotic cell," which appears in the fossil record roughly a billion-and-a-half years after the first lifeforms made their appearance on this planet. The eukaryotic cell rose to become the dominant lifeform at the outset of the Proterozoic Eon because of geological driving forces which continually stressed and altered the Earth's ecosystem.

The fossil record tells us that the very first lifeforms on Earth appeared early in the Archean Eon, perhaps as early as four billion years ago, at a time when environmental conditions were extremely hostile. After the mantle had crystallized, and after the crust had cooled and hardened, the Earth's surface was frequently rent, melted and re-melted by massive volcanic eruptions. Later, volatiles outgassed through great fissures and returned to the Earth's surface in torrents of rainfall. Between 4.6 and about 4.0 BYA the Earth's surface was bombarded by comets and asteroids, providing an additional source of water and volatiles. At the end of the period of meteorite bombardment, the Earth's surface had grown extremely hot, steamy, and foreboding. Rainwater usually contained H_2SO_4 (sulfuric acid), which accumulated in shallow lowland pools where the pH was somewhere between intolerable and ridiculous. All the while, the Earth's raging volcanism supplied a steady stream of sulfur, carbon dioxide, and juvenile water to supplement the other components of outgassing. At some point in time after the crust had become stable, and after a hydrologic cycle had been initiated, portions of the fragile crust began to break down and erode, and sedimentation began. The onset of sedimentation and the formation of oceans are well-documented in the geologic record (Foster, "Historical Geology," p. 128):

> By about 4000 million years ago, the crust had formed. By 3800 million years ago, the ocean and atmosphere probably were present because water-deposited sedimentary rocks of this age have been found...[36]

Some scientists associate the advent of life on Earth with the period of meteorite bombardment that occurred soon after the planet's formation, and which occurred about the same time as the onset of sedimentation. They suggest that life may therefore have an extraterrestrial origin. The available evidence neither fully confirms nor denies this increasingly popular theory. However, many biologists continue to believe that life originated as a by-product of the complex chemistry of the primeval Earth.

By roughly 3.8 billion years ago, shallow, expansive oceans occupied most of the Earth's surface. These "epeiric" seas, as they are often called by geologists, seem to have encompassed about 85 or 90 percent of the surface, and probably formed the first real habitat. *Primitive* **archaebacteria** *appear in the geological record about 3.8 billion years ago, after the early epeiric seas had already formed. Curiously, the appearance of archaebacteria coincides with the appearance of the first sedimentary deposits*, as noted by Paul Strother (article "Pre-Metazoan Life" from "Evolution and the Fossil Record"):

> ...The recognition of iron formation and metaquartzite in the supracrustals from Isua, Western Greenland, clearly indicate that the hydrologic cycle existed 3800-3900 Myr ago... sedimentary rocks from the Pilbara Block of western Australia clearly indicate the existence of shallow-water habitats 3450 Myr ago...[37]

It is clear, then, that the first lifeforms made their appearance at or about the time of the appearance of sediments, both on our planet and on Mars (assuming that the existence of NASA's fossilized Martian bacteria is ultimately confirmed). The possibility that sedimentation somehow spurred the development of the first lifeforms is increasingly supported by geochemical research. German theoretical chemist Gunter Waechtershaeuser suggests that life began as a series of chemical reactions between key organic molecules found in the mineral "pyrite." Pyrite surfaces have a positive charge that could attract and polymerize negatively charged organophosphates, perhaps causing them to unzip from their phosphate coating to become free organic molecules and possible precursors of life.

Waechtershaeuser and other geochemists have also found that chemicals crucial to cell metabolism can be produced by interactions between rock formed from deep-seated magma and gases common to the primordial Earth. From experiments, Waechtershaeuser has developed a theory that he has termed "The Iron Sulfur World Theory," suggesting: (1) that metabolitic processes occurred naturally in the Earth's early inanimate environment, (2) that these processes came into being from reactions catalyzed by the metallic surfaces of iron sulfides such as pyrite, and (3) that these were later programmed into the chemistry of complex non-living molecules. The theory strongly suggests that these same processes were later incorporated into living cells via the development of primitive RNA/DNA. Fundamental to this theory is the notion that "autocatalysis" emerged as a natural chemical process in the early Earth, a process in which the products of a reaction enable the reaction, itself, to go faster. Waechtershaeuser suggests that life may have originated from autocatalytic processes which generated lipids, a fatty chemical, that subsequently enclosed an autocatalytic chemical system with metabolic features.

A.G. Cairns-Smith of the University of Glasgow (Scotland) believes that the riddle of life is intimately tied to ordinary clay. This is an old notion that has been expressed in the scientific literature for decades. I can recall one of my geology professors meticulously developing this argument in an environmental geology class I took in 1974, and the idea itself is surely much older than that. How can this be? Mineralogically, clay is an extremely fine-grained "sheet silicate." Sheet silicates are chemically bound together into an elongated silica-oxygen string, typically incorporating aluminum, iron, magnesium and other cations of similar size and valency to chemically neutralize the prevailing negative charge of the sheet silicate. The resulting structure of these layered sheets is very grossly similar to that of genetic material, implying that organophosphates and proteins involved in autocatalysis may have used the sheet as a mold or supporting structure in forming the first RNA/DNA fragments. Cairns-Smith notes that clay minerals can act as a template and absorb organic molecules, catalyze their breakdown, and synthesize them into other substances. He has also speculated that innate imperfections in the microscopic structure of clay may have been passed on, imprinting primitive RNA (and DNA) with the seeds of genetic variation. This line of thought suggests that the diversity of our biosphere may be a byproduct of innate variations in the sheet structure of clay. By whatever mechanism, life was clearly shaped and molded during the early Archean. Whether this occurred via pyrite, clay, and/or in association with the mineralogy of the classical warm, bubbly "Darwin Pond" is simply unknown.

What is known is that the geologic record contains clear evidence of microbes at 3.8 billion years ago, and it is certain that these were not the first lifeforms. The first lifeforms probably go as far back as 4.2 or 4.3 billion years ago, and would likely have been little more than snippets of genetic material enclosed within lipids and/or organic tissue. Perhaps tiny, primitive microbacteria formed from this process and branched out along separate lines early in the Earth's history. The survival of primitive lifeforms in the Earth's early, hyper-hostile environment would almost certainly have been a touch-and-go proposition. A growing number of biologists suggest that life began first on the relatively cooler and more hospitable Mars (which was quite warm and wet during the planet's early history), and then traveled to Earth within the belly of one or more Martian meteorites. A number of credible studies have found this to be a very plausible idea. An inevitable result of exposure to the primordial Earth, however, was the evolution of hardy *archaebacteria* known as "extremophiles," which are the first fossilized cells appearing in the geologic record (at 3.8 BYA). *Extremophiles* have modern descendants which remain uniquely suited to survival in hot, acidic pools like those of the early Archean—and which can still thrive in conditions that would quickly kill modern bacteria and protozoans.

The purported finding by NASA scientists of primitive, fossilized microbacteria in Martian rocks (rocks that made their way to Antarctica via meteorites) is potentially one of the most intriguing discoveries of our day. These tiny, supposed "Martians" seem to have originated at a time when the red planet was warm and had an active hydrologic cycle, and active sedimentation. Could it be that autocatalysis and DNA-molding first occurred on Mars, and that early Martian organisms made their way to Earth during the period of meteorite bombardment in the early Archean? No one yet knows. The purported Martians, however, have been dated at 4.5 billion years in age, which makes them possible progenitors of Earthian archaebacteria, and perhaps throwbacks to the earliest conceivable lifeforms in our stellar system. The fact that the biggest of these microfossils was only 200 nanometers (one billionth of a meter times 200) means that these purported creatures are little more than tiny snippets of RNA engulfed in a shell of lipids and organic material— precisely what we might expect of the first lifeforms. The tiniest known microbacteria currently living on Earth are roughly three times the size of these creatures. And, it is clear that the Red Planet (red because of iron) would provide adequate resources for an "Iron-Sulfur World."

The importance of all this for the *God Theory* is that it constitutes scientific evidence in support of evolution. It strongly suggests that life emerged from the sediments, and Waechtershaeuser's theory has answered many of the questions about how this might have happened. The purported Martian microfossils, despite controversy, remain a credible find, especially since they were found in deposits of calcium carbonate like that formed chemically along the warm coastlines of Earth—which serve a natural incubator of life. In every scenario, life becomes a product of the sediments. **Coincidentally, Genesis 3:19 tells us that: *"...dust thou art and to dust thou shalt return."*** We are further told in Genesis 2:7 that: *"The Lord God made man from the dust of the ground, and 'breathed into his nostrils the breath of life', and man became a living soul."*

In the movie *Adam and Eve*, we are led to envision an almost instantaneous creation of the first man. The movie creates an idyllic setting in which God suddenly whips up a windstorm and fashions Adam into a living being from nothing more than swirling eddies of dust. However, this "Hollywood duststorm hypothesis" is by no means what the Bible reports. Genesis simply states that *"God MADE man from the dust of the ground"*! It doesn't say precisely how this process occurred, or how long it took. The windstorm is nothing more than a product of rich Hollywood imagination, and sustains my earlier contentions that scripture usually doesn't provide sufficient detail, and that human imagination will be used to fill in the gaps in scripture if science is cast aside and ignored! The analyses conducted in this book totally refute any notion that the creation of Adam might have occurred within the duration of a 24-hour day.

Careful reading of the Second and Third Chapters of Genesis turns up nothing at all that is preclusive of a much slower, deliberative and evolutionary process. It is exactly this sort of process that is implicated in Waechtershaeuser's "Iron-Sulfur World Theory," the ideas of Cairns-Smith about clay, and the discovery of the Martian microfossils announced by NASA. These convergent theories and findings seem to confirm what scientists have long suspected—that life progressed very slowly from tiny and simple unicellular forms to forms that are much more complex, over billions of years. This progression, in reality, begins not at the time when life began, but at the time of the Big Bang, when the process of the chemical evolution of the universe began. The accumulating weight of evidence suggests an evolutionary process managed by the de-facto "Hand of God," which is physically manifested in our universe by the force of gravity. To be explicit, I am openly contending that God and gravity are one, and that God is truly an intelligent, living force manifested in the shaping forces of gravity, as well as in other forces of nature, and matter. God created through evolution!

When we come to this understanding and affirm the doctrine of theistic evolution, conflict between science and scripture evaporates. Open-minded analysis of the scriptures, set in their proper cultural, philosophical and historical context, only sustains this conclusion, for nothing scripturally or theologically precludes evolution as the process by which God created everything. As nature evolved, God may simply have spurred geological and environmental changes which gradually evolved the simple into the complex, or He may have pre-ordained everything via the mix of matter and energy inherent in the Big Bang. In every respect, then, our lineage is both progressive and reversible. God caused it all to happen naturally, the only question is the extent of His direct involvement in the various creative phases. In the end, the hubbub of fundamentalists about evolution amounts to much ado about nothing. Theistic evolution is not atheistic.

I believe that all denominations should take the same view on this issue as the Roman Catholics, who, under the leadership of Pope John Paul II, have given open arms to the doctrine of Theistic Evolution. Evolution is the only concept that makes sense of everything that we can see in the natural environment, including ourselves. It tells us that microbacteria evolved into heat-and-salt-loving *extremophiles* (examples of which are still alive today), and that these are ancestral to all of Earth's lifeforms. It tells that, in time, these produced a prokaryotic cellular lineage which later gave rise to eukaryotes, from which higher lifeforms emerged. The fossil record and biological evidence tells us that prokaryotes were protected from chemical oxidation and unshielded solar, ultraviolet radiation by thick cellular walls, a feature which accounts for their pre-eminence during the mid- to late-Archean. They, of course, came into being and thrived under anaerobic conditions, and their composition protected them from exposure to oxygen—which would have oxidized and destroyed them. Rising oxygen levels, changing climatic conditions and changing patterns of nutrient dispersal due to continental drift and supercontinental accretion slowly gave rise to the more advanced and variable eukaryotes. As these creatures proliferated, many of them processed carbon dioxide into oxygen via photosynthesis and began to play a major role in oxygenating the atmosphere. As oxygen levels increased, cells grew larger, more dynamic and increasingly complex.

Oxygen is the most plentiful of the elements in the earth's crust, having a weight percentage of almost 47 percent of the crustal mass, and accounting for fully 60% of the individual atoms in the crust. Hundreds of minerals have formed "oxides" by chemical bonding with oxygen. While great reserves of oxygen have always been tied up in the Earth's geochemistry, prior to the late Proterozoic Eon (about one billion years ago) only tiny amounts had been freed into the primitive atmosphere.

The geologic record tells us that large and complex eukaryotic creatures began to emerge only after the Earth's atmosphere was oxygenated to about one-twentieth of its current level. One of the great issues of science over the last half century is the reason why oxygen levels increased from less than one percent of current levels at 1.9 billion years ago, to about six percent by roughly 700 million years ago. How is it, in other words, that environmental conditions favored a 500 percent increase in oxygen levels within a timespan of only 1.2 billion years?

Studies of remanent magnetism in igneous rocks over the past few decades have increasingly linked atmospheric oxygenation to geological processes, not the least of which is continual supercontinental accretion and breakup. The geologic record suggests that after the breakup of the Early Proterozoic Supercontinent, a "Late Proterozoic Supercontinent" appeared briefly at about 1.2 billion years ago. This landmass apparently broke apart, subdivided, then reassembled about 700 or 800 million years ago, forming a new supercontinent that geologists have dubbed "*Rodinia*." Rodinia, in turn, later broke into two sub-units which are recognized as direct antecedents of our modern continental landmasses. The northernmost of these sub-units has been called "Laurasia," while the southernmost and largest is termed "Gondwana."

Incessant coupling and de-coupling of *Laurasia* and *Gondwana* seems to have provided a major driving force for the release of oxygen into the atmosphere. In our ecological system, the amount of oxygen generated is balanced by the amount that is consumed by biological and geological processes. Such activities include respiration, weathering, and oxidation of chemically reduced gases given off by organisms and volcanoes (Knoll):

> Only when the amount of oxygen released during photosynthesis exceeds the amount consumed by oxidation will oxygen levels increase... Oxygen levels are most likely to rise not when more photosynthetic matter is produced but when more is buried in sediments... If oxygen levels increased during that period (the late Proterozoic), we could expect to find the increase reflected in higher rates of organic carbon burial.[38]

Armed with this hypothesis, Knoll and other scientists conducted tests of carbon isotopes which affirmed that organic carbon had been buried at an unusually rapid rate all throughout the late Proterozoic. Tests using strontium isotopes suggested strong hydrothermal activity in the oceans during this same time interval. A correlation between carbon burial and tectonic activity soon became clear cut. Carbon burial was seen as the obvious result of supercontinental accretion, breakup and associated processes. Simply stated, the formation and breakup of the Rodinian Supercontinent seems to have deep-buried immense amounts of organic carbon, and this, in turn, increased the oxidizing potential of the atmosphere and hydrosphere. Minerals such as hematite (Fe_2O_3) with iron in an Fe^{+3} form were produced from oxidation reactions, dissolved (liquid) iron then disappeared, and oceans became supersaturated with oxygen and with the aid of resulting blooms of algae began to release it into the atmosphere. The resulting oxygenation was just enough to allow complex eukaryotes to branch out into (and form) the first tiny, primitive metazoan (multicellular) creatures, and to allow these to get over the hump, and to form immense blankets of green algae and eventually phytoplankton along the ocean surface. By 700 million years ago, atmospheric oxygen levels were about one-tenth of the current levels. By 600 million years ago, truly complex metazoan creatures are clearly indicated in the fossil record. By the onset of the Cambrian Period (i.e. the Paleozoic Era, Phanerozoic Eon), which is now placed at about 543 million years ago, oxygen levels had attained about half to two-thirds that of current atmospheric levels, a level sufficient to allow the veritable "explosion" of lifeforms (termed the "Ediacaran Radiation") that we can clearly see in the fossil record, and which formed the basis of the Earth's modern ecosystem.

We see in this analysis the perpetual and unceasing impact of the Earth's geological driving forces upon the emergence of life and the evolution of higher lifeforms. During the earliest portions of the Paleozoic Era, life quickly differentiated. Trilobites (shelly, seafaring arthropods) and Brachiopods (clamlike creatures) entered the fossil record during the early *Cambrian* Period. True vertebrates (in the form of primitive fish) appeared in the later Cambrian, and by the end of the Cambrian, all of the modern phyla (major subdivisions of life) had appeared. During the subsequent *Ordovician* Period (505-438 MYA) lifeforms further branched out, became more complex and more abundant. Then:

> It was some 430 million years ago, during the Silurian Period, that plants appear to have emerged from the sea and established themselves on land. The early Devonian land plants, while small and simple were widely distributed: they ranged from the Falkland Islands to Spitsbergen to the interior of Asia and North America.[39]

The emergence and proliferation of plantlife on dry land was clearly one of the most profound events in the history of our planet, forming an essential link in the food chain for land creatures and further accelerating atmospheric oxygenation. It should come as no surprise that this major event is also recorded in Genesis 1:11:

> 11. Then God said, "Let the earth bring forth grass, the herb that yields seed, and the fruit tree that yields fruit according to its kind, whose seed is in itself, on the earth, and it was so.[40]

The appearance of plantlife on land, followed by the appearance of lungfish and amphibians (20-40 million years later) effectively prepped our world for the subsequent appearance of reptiles and mammals. Again, supercontinental accretion played a major role in the evolution of our ecosystem. The accretion of the Pangaean Supercontinent about 210 million years ago created a massive hot, dry tropical and sub-tropical desert, parts of which were separated from the moderating influences of the ocean by thousands of miles. The horrendous pressures of this caustic environment favored the development of creatures with scaly, protective skin whose eggs would gestate on dry land—i.e. reptiles. Dinosaurs later appeared from this lineage and flourished long enough for one distinct family, the "theropods" to give rise to birds. Mammals developed from ancestors of the dinosaurs, and shared the Earth with them during the Mesozoic as a subservient species.

A theory that the Earth was struck by a giant asteroid about 65 million years ago, killing the dinosaurs and causing a mass extinction, is sustained by: (1) a worldwide layer of the rare element "iridium" at the boundary between the Cretaceous and the Tertiary geologic periods—Iridium is an element which is almost exclusively found in meteorites and deep inside planets; and (2) a giant crater in the Caribbean just off Mexico's Yucatan Peninsula. This collision appears to have thrown up a giant cloud of dust and debris, and later caused raging forest fires which threw up huge clouds of smoke. Massive amounts of dust and smoke then collected in the stratosphere and obscured the sun for years after the collision. During this time period, green plants were deprived of sunlight and died out, and this led to the starvation of plant-eating dinosaurs and the giant carnivores that fed upon the herbivores. The surviving land fauna consisted primarily of insects that fed upon dead vegetation and creatures that fed upon the insects—i.e., warm-blooded mammalian creatures, and birds.

On the whole, it is clear that life has advanced from the simplest to the most complex forms in tiny, definitive evolutionary steps, and with the sole exception of the asteroid collision that wiped out the dinosaurs, major changes in the Earth's ecosystem seem always to have been prompted by geological driving forces. However, gravity has been involved as a major driving force for change in each and every instance. Genesis only provides a broad summary of the key events that helped to constitute our ecosystem. Science vastly expands the available information about these events. The key scientific-scriptural composites impacting the Earth's ecosystem are: (1) the formation and re-formation of world-oceans and supercontinents via plate tectonics; (2) the notion that life originated in the "dust of the Earth"; and (3) a progression of lifeforms from the relatively simple to the increasingly complex. Science and scripture correlate on all of these points. The overall evidence tells us that biological evolution is just a small portion of a much larger process of physical evolution, which ultimately ties large and sophisticated creatures like ourselves to the Big Bang, eternity, and God.

Our conclusion is that gravity amounts to the creative hand of God. It either constitutes evidence of God, or it is God, Himself. Gravity *caused the condensation of the first simple atoms after the Big Bang and gave the universe its initial (as well as final) structure. It gave us, in succession, atoms, gasclouds, protogalaxies, suns, new elements, our galaxy, and ultimately our own solar system. It then caused our planet to accrete, solidified its crust and caused its tectonic plates to form. It then kept those plates in motion, and in so doing gradually transformed the Earth's surface into a suitable place for life. Once life appeared, gravity provided for the organization of microtubules in the cytoskeleton of developing cells, without which cellular apparatus could not have taken on essential form and pattern. Without gravity, the beautiful place that we call our universe would not exist, and there would be no lifeforms to observe the universe and carry on a debate about its origin. Indeed, gravity has created most of what the scriptures ascribe to The Almighty. Having recognized this, perhaps we shall move on to a more in-depth exploration of gravity, and then God.*

CHAPTER SEVEN

SO WHAT IS PERFECTION?

A bit of synthesis is appropriate before we move on. Thus far, we have seen that literalism embraces archaic notions such as the Ptolemaic Model, which are totally inappropriate for the world of the 21st Century. We have also seen that the Bible did not descend from heaven surrounded by cherubim, that it was created by man, that portions of it (especially the Old Testament) have been substantially edited and revised, and that it sometimes contains error—always as a result of human editing and distillation. While scripture is not perfect, there is vast evidence of direct and subtle messages that sometimes run profoundly parallel to those of science, and which suggest a Divine Origin.

The earliest scriptures show that the "Elohists" disagreed with the "Yahwists" about the importance of Jerusalem in Hebrew worship, and that there were major differing views between early Hebrew tribes and religious sects on the nature of the covenant between God and Israel—the issue was whether that covenant had been made with just a few select leaders, such as Moses and Joshua (as believed by the Yahwists), or with the entire Hebrew Nation (as believed by the Elohists). From this general disagreement and the separation of the Hebrew State into distinct northern and southern kingdoms arise opposing messages at the outset of the scriptures, and a clear indication that the very earliest "word" was oral in tradition, and not universally agreed upon. The written word—when it finally appeared—only exacerbated the existing divisions, and this led to countless efforts to shape and reshape the word to fit various definitions of truth. Were this not the case, we would not be able to

113

trace the clear and unmistakable lines of *Elohist and Yahwist thought that exists in the Bible*, and there would be far fewer resulting scriptural contradictions. The scriptures thus originated in controversy, and never quite lost it. As a result, they were often subject to revision to reflect the views of new priestly and political groups which had risen to power, and new and unique theological perspectives arising from new knowledge about the world, or contact with new cultures and ideas. The *Deuteronomists* and *Hebrew Priests of Babylon* were not necessarily in disagreement with earlier genre on key issues, theirs was instead an effort to explain something that seemed to defy the covenant between God and Israel—why a God of resounding power Who had freed the Hebrews from the clutches of a mighty Egyptian Pharaoh would continually allow them to be overrun and enslaved by surrounding nations. Theirs was a quest to link the recurrent destruction of the Hebrew State to the recurrent abandonment of the law by the Hebrew peoples. To this quest, they introduced ideas which would inevitably place the scriptures out-of-sync with Psalms 19:1 and modern science.

God is not the author of scriptural error. The existence of four distinct theological, Old Testament genres is testimony to the intervention of man, and to the impact of human double-distillation. In scrutinizing the four separate rabbinical influences it becomes obvious that much of the Old Testament was profoundly influenced by politics, history and culture. It contains human additions attesting to this in addition to Divine Revelation. The human additions, however, must not be allowed to obscure the contributions of the Divine, for the Old Testament is replete with messages that run profoundly parallel to those of science; and when interpreted from a scientific perspective, new meaning is quick to emerge. It is my belief that the gist of the biblical message meets the requirements of Jefferson and Paine—harmony between God's Creation and the nature that we can observe scientifically. The "light correlation," for example, profoundly links Genesis 1:3 with the Big Bang Theory, and also with Einstein's Theory of Special Relativity.

Linkage between text written in the Ninth Century B.C. and

modern science cannot be easily explained away, and is suggestive of a Divine origin. While such linkages ought to provide rich fodder for theological interpretation, we need only look around us and read the newspapers to determine that most such linkages are instead ignored because of existing interpretive traditions that are highly literalistic. Modern theology, based as it is upon a partial Pre-Copernican view of the universe, largely ignores the real and potential connections of science to theology. Science is thus deprived of a rightful and appropriate impact upon theology, and ultimately it is the message of the Bible that suffers. Instead, we are forced to live with the scathing medieval theology of fire-breathing literalists and conservatives, who seem altogether *hell-bent* on ignoring the potential of science for opening the scriptures to more substantive meaning. Yet, all that has been achieved in the name of biblical preservation is a watered-down, paradoxical, inconsistent version of theology that we have difficulty associating with the world around us. Under the vast flowing banners of biblical literalism, the fundamentalists implicitly ignore: (1) the ancient bad science used by ancient priests and scribes to create the prevailing theology that we have inherited, (2) the lessons of history, and (3) the power of modern science.

Modern Christian evangelical traditions are devoted to the spread of the gospel of Jesus Christ and have little concern with the elimination of paradox in Old Testament theology. The result is that theologians who keep pushing literalism are increasingly pushing forward into the future with a genre of thought and theology that is increasingly outdated. At risk is the entire system of Judeo-Christian beliefs, for too much new scientific information is accumulating to sustain traditional literalism. The "revealed religions" will either be updated, or in time they will be swept away.

Scriptural dynamism is the way out of this mindless cycle of traditional influences and ignorance. While no one idea can dismantle all that is archaic and wrong, scriptural dynamism provides an interpretive tool that rational, open-minded leaders of all denominations can use to correct past error. It can and must be used to strike down needless walls erected between science and theology, which preclude theologians and their flocks from a deeper understanding of God, our universe, and the great caissons of eternity. Scriptural dynamism is a modern, theological naturalism that allows scripture to open and bloom—in synch with the flowering of human knowledge.

The *God Theory* is based on a series of grand composites of science and scripture that harmonize one with the other. In succession, these tell us: that all matter was in the form of a black hole before the moment of creation, that God's creation of light in Genesis 1:3 was followed by the rumble of the Big Bang, that the light of the Big Bang heralded in the words "Let there be light..." created the matter of the universe; and that the appearance of gravity as the first of the great forces of nature extended the "Hand of God" into the universe and steered creation from the moment of the Big Bang to the here-and-now, from creation processes on a grand scale that built the galaxies and the over-riding structure of the universe, to creation on a fine scale that gave the universe complex chemistry, and ultimately life.

From a grand composite of science and scripture, gravity comes to us as the most important player in the process of creation. The mechanisms of gravity and the other great forces of nature explain how the universe came into being, and how nature was shaped to its current form. We can see it at work not only in the heavens (via astronomy and astrophysics), but also in our own world (via geology, geophysics and biology). Before the Earth was formed, gravity built our universe, galaxy and solar system. After the Earth was formed, it became the driving force behind geological processes which, in turn, engineered a slow-but-steady evolution of our ecosystem, culminating in ourselves. The composite of science and Genesis suggests the existence of a God Who intimately planned Creation before He caused it to happen, for there was but one creative event and its components had to be precisely orchestrated.

The precision of this grand event, the Big Bang, does not suggest the existence of a Creator who would do dumb things like creating plants before sunlight, which the literal sequence of "creation days" in Genesis would have us believe. Biblical paradox must be seen for what it really is, a product that God would not give us, and the inevitable result of hasty, often short-sighted scriptural editing.

The Bible may tell us about God, and give us a recipe for connecting with Him, but it was written by hands connected to ancient minds and it cannot convey an understanding of modern science or of God's *physical nature*. It tells instead of God's basic characteristics—omniscience, omnipotence, omnipresence, and immutability—but it doesn't tell us how or why a "spirit" might possess such attributes. When the Bible was written, there was no way to deal with such issues. Today we have better tools to explain the nature of God. In ancient Israel at the time the scriptures were written, concepts and theories essential to an understanding of God were not yet in existence.

We are about to engage the tools of modern science to explain the existence of God and draw the *God Theory* to its logical conclusion. A new view of God will emerge over the next few pages. The reader should understand, here and now, that we will not end this book with a vision of some grand old bearded fellow with sharp eyes, reposing eternally upon a Great White Throne. The *God Theory* will paint a very different portrait—of a Deity Who is at one with the universe, Who is also a living persona, and Who inherently understands our deepest thoughts, emotions and limitations. He understands because He is integral to all of it. Many theologians would contend that it is improper to focus on the physical nature of God without also focusing upon God's persona, and what He wants for us. I have no objection to this. So, what does God want from us? I believe that John Calvin was right in his view that God, more than anything else, wants an enduring relationship. As we shall see in the next few pages, God has built a relationship with us against incredible barriers. God, by His very nature, is inaccessible to us! We cannot see Him, touch Him, or carry on a conversation with Him. He occupies a different realm of creation than us. ***We are physical beings, and God is virtual.*** The complete meaning of this will come later. To bridge the great gulf that separates us from Him, God has carefully staked out the evidence of His being. The universe is that evidence—its beauty, its great forces, its vastness, and its eternal relevance. God has also planted evidence of His being in people—the prophets, a messiah (as some believe), ministers, doctors, scientists, all those who do God's work. We can see God in Copernicus, Galileo, and Einstein—individuals who have given us hope and vision, and who have wrestled science from the grip of reactionaries. We can see God in the lives of moralistic leaders—people as diverse and strikingly human as Billy Graham and Pope John Paul II.

But truly "seeing God" is going to be disquieting to some. The great *coin of irreconciliation has two sides—one occupied by literalists and hard-core fundamentalists, and the other by atheistic scientists! Both strongly oppose scientific-scriptural reconciliation and scoff at any notion that science and scripture correlate, or that composites of science and scripture may be valid. We have dealt with literalism, and now is the time to view* the other side of the coin.

Many scientists embraced atheism and/or agnosticism after Copernicus and Galileo, and during the "Age of Rationalism." The cause of atheism (or agnosticism) was given further boost by Darwinism and the Steady State Theory, and by incessant bickering between scientists and fundamentalist theologians. Though the Big Bang Theory ultimately shifted the weight of evidence away from the notion of a "perpetual creation" and toward the notion of a "finite moment of creation," (strengthening the case for a "Divine Creation") it is by no means correct to say that strict adherence to the Big Bang Theory leads automatically to belief in God. Nothing could sometimes be farther from the truth.

Many scientists adhere to the Big Bang Theory, today, while holding tenaciously to a view that the Big Bang was only a chance event, an event utterly devoid of religious implications. An increasingly powerful and recognizable scientific following has gathered around *the notion of a chance creation, and a philosophical doctrine called "Anthropism."* The "anthropists" argue that because all of creation seems to have been perfectly calibrated *to output ourselves*, we only naturally tend to believe that everything was created by a God Who has a marvelous plan for us. Our innate tendency to see our own existence as miraculous and Divine is, they say, nothing more than typical human fallacy. *They contend that the universe, in truth, is nothing more than a chance product of an accidental event*—that some chance event, or series of chance events, somehow started the universe down the long road of physical evolution, and that we are the result of that process. As might be expected, their beliefs are predicated on a reasonably sound interpretation of scientific facts, and application of well-developed philosophical notions that can be difficult for a non-scientist to refute.

More than anything else, anthropism is an offshoot of "quantum mechanics," and so to approach an understanding of anthropism one must at least have a cursory qualitative understanding of quantum mechanics. "Quantum mechanics" unfolded during the very early 1900s as a distinct branch of physics, with immediate and stunning impacts upon science and technology. However, its influence on human philosophy and everyday thought took longer to develop. Though it has intensely powerful things to say about the fundamental nature of the universe, its tenets are often difficult to formulate in everyday language. Though it is a regular in scientific publications, college campuses and research centers, it seldom makes the agenda of discussion groups, civic clubs, and churches. As a result, its philosophical applications have been substantially confined to intellectual circles. Physicists, astronomers, astrophysicists, and chemists have been profoundly influenced by quantum mechanics, but not sociologists, historians and theologians. The so-called "anthropic principle," which dominates the philosophy of the anthropists, can be traced to a group of physicists led by Stephen Hawking. This circle includes some of the world's most revered scientists and greatest minds. On the whole, they see our universe as little more than a vast "incubator" of life, an incubator that coincidentally happens to reflect the creation processes preconditional to the output of humanity. Anthropism is a unique and sometimes curiously reverential philosophy. The fact that our universe survived the "big bang" is regarded as a profound marvel (Hawking):

...The initial rate of expansion also would have had to be chosen very precisely for the rate of expansion still to be so close to the critical rate needed to avoid recollapse. This means that the initial state of the universe must have been very carefully chosen indeed if the hot big bang model was correct right back to the beginning of time. It would be very difficult to explain why the universe should have begun in just this way, except as the act of a God who intended to create beings like us.[41]

Detailed study of Hawking, however, reveals that the foregoing does not amount to an affirmation of the existence of God. *Perfection by Divine Plan is only a comparative tool that Hawking uses to emphasize the fact that random process does occasionally engender precision and perfection.* He (and other scientists) frequently illustrate this principle with what I would call *"the parable of the typing monkeys,"* which goes something like this: Give one monkey a typewriter, and it will type out predictable garbage. The same is true of ten monkeys, a hundred, a million, a billion, or perhaps a *gazillion*; but give out enough typewriters and enough paper to enough monkeys, over a long-enough period of time, and then one marvelous day one of them will just happen to type out one of Shakespeare's sonnets—purely by accident! The law of probability, in other words, becomes the singular controlling force in our universe. Given enough time and enough repetition, just about anything can happen. The seemingly miraculous nature of the creation process ("Brief History" p. 125) is only an example of the power of probability, and the ultimate validity of the anthropic principle:

The laws of science, as we know them at present, contain many fundamental numbers, like the size of the electric charge of the electron and the ratio of the masses of the proton and the electron. We cannot, at the moment at least, predict the values of these numbers from theory—we have to find them by observation... The remarkable fact is that the values of these numbers seem to have been very finely adjusted to make possible the development of life. For example, if the electric charge of the electron had been only slightly different, stars either would have been unable to burn hydrogen and helium, or else they would not have exploded. Of course, there might be other forms of intelligent life, not dreamed of even by writers of science fiction, that did not require the light of a star like the sun or the heavier chemical elements that are made in stars and are flung back into space when the stars explode.

Nevertheless, it seems clear that there are relatively few ranges of values for the numbers that would allow the development of any form of intelligent life. Most sets of values would give rise to universes that, although they might be very beautiful, would contain no one able to wonder at that beauty. One can take this either as evidence of a divine purpose in Creation and the choice of the laws of science or as support for the strong anthropic principle.[42]

Physicist Brandon Carter, who formulated the "Anthropic Principle" (and who was one of Stephen Hawking's early associates) uses anthropism in his own writing to illustrate the fact that we *inherently tend to see in creation the processes necessary for our own existence and survival. An implicit suggestion of anthropism is that we have a strong, innate, natural bias that causes us to misinterpret facts.* The anthropists insist that we inevitably fool ourselves into believing that everything has proceeded, lockstep, from the beginning of time, as if there was some sort of grand plan for the output of human beings. Since everyone knows that our existence is fragile and finite, they say, it is only natural for us to see ourselves as a miraculous culmination of divinely orchestrated events. They, themselves, recognize the marvel of our existence, and that recognition permeates their own descriptive language. Greenstein, for example, builds the notion of perfection-of-process to a crescendo, and the result sounds like something that might be heard in a sermon or a Sunday school class:

> ...the density of the universe could have been no greater than eight times the critical density (to avoid recollapse)... 1 million years after the big bang it was no more than one-third of 1 percent greater than critical density (to avoid recollapse)... one year after creation, it was no more than 0.00003 percent denser than critical... When the universe was one hour old it could have exceeded critical density by no more than 0.00000008 percent; the slightest deviation would have caused it to recollapse essentially at once.
>
> ..In the limit, we come face to face with the inconceivable, the unfathomable: the moment of creation itself. Suddenly we know something about it. It was such as to allow the present configuration of the cosmos ultimately to arise, and this required an adjustment not of one part in a thousand, not of one part in a trillion, but of one part in *infinity*. CREATION WAS PERFECT.[43]

But what is perfection? Is it something ordained only by God, that relates only to Him, or is it something that has achieved every detail of what seems appropriate for our existence, purely by chance? To me, for creation to have been perfect, the probability of the universe forming by accident would also seem to be infinitely small. The smaller the probability (i.e. the greater the number of zeroes after the decimal place), the greater the likelihood that creation can only be seen as miraculous in nature. But, anthropists suggest that the probability of this occurrence is fully explained by the "parable of the typing monkeys." Rather than endorsing the idea of a Divine Creation, as I half-expected after a naive first reading of Greenstein,

I found him adept at 180-degree turns, after which he back-flipped, and suddenly came up with a statement that I at first found utterly confusing: "*...creation was only perfect with respect to the anthropic principle.*" He then retreated into what seemed like "metaphysics" with the following pronouncement (p. 223, "The Symbiotic Universe"):

> The argument of this and the preceding chapter is that in the fitness for life of the cosmos we are witnessing the effects of a gigantic symbiosis, a symbiosis between the universe on the one hand and life on the other. THE PROPOSAL IS THAT THE COSMOS BROUGHT FORTH LIFE IN ORDER TO EXIST. The first half of the argument is now complete: It is that in order for a single particle to exist, it must be observed. In the present chapter two additional steps will be taken. The first is to argue that what is true of a single particle is also true of collections of particles: stones, planets— even the universe as a whole. THE IMPLICATION IS THAT THE VERY COSMOS DOES NOT EXIST UNLESS OBSERVED. AND the second step will be THAT ONLY A CONSCIOUS MIND IS CAPABLE OF PERFORMING SUCH AN OBSERVATION.[44]

Greenstein begins the concluding chapter of his book by calling quantum mechanics a "great revolution in thought." He then proceeds to establish the "anthropic principle" as a philosophical by-product of quantum mechanics. The link between the two is, in fact, implicit in the foregoing quotation, which asserts that the cosmos requires observation in order to exist. Greenstein's assertion relates directly to Heisenberg's famous "*Uncertainty Principle.*"

In 1926, the German physicist Werner Heisenberg outlined a fundamental principle explaining why it is inherently impossible to precisely predict the position of an electron at any one instant in time. Heisenberg's many experiments had found that when a photon of light strikes an electron, the electron always goes reeling off into space, along a new trajectory. Successive attempts to gain a precise fix on the electron by hitting it with a beam of light are always doomed to the same result. In effect, each effort to "see" (an electron) only "distorts" its location by scattering it into parts unknown. The more one attempts to see the electron, to get a fix on its position in space, the more one only bombards it with photons and compounds the uncertainty of its position. Heisenberg therefore demonstrated that there is always a certain degree of uncertainty in any prediction about the position of any sub-atomic particle. That uncertainty, he noted, could never be smaller than a quantity known as "Planck's Constant," which is a tiny factor used in concert with light-speed and light-wavelength to predict changes in energy states of atoms. Its value of 6.626×10^{-34} is fixed and never changes.

So it is that in quantum mechanics, the existence of a sub-atomic particle at a given location is always profoundly affected by: (1) an effort to observe, and (2) basic probability theory. *Similarly, Greenstein's universe is profoundly affected by an effort to observe. It can only exist IF there are intelligent beings around to observe it. At the same time, Greenstein suggests that the entire universe behaves in accordance with the laws of quantum mechanics, and that "...what is true of a single particle is also true of collections of particles: stones, planets—even the universe as a whole...,"* This is much of the philosophical basis of what Hawking has termed the "quantum universe," and just by chance it provides some of the logic needed to complete the *God Theory*, as I will show later.

In an important sense, the anthropic principle is a major strike against the principle of "determinism." Determinism was an idea set forth in the early 19th century by the French scientist the Marquis de Laplace, who argued that there should be some set of scientific laws which would allow us to determine and predict every event in the universe, if only we knew the laws and the state of the universe at any one point in time. Scientific determinism was resisted, at the time of Laplace, by theologians who clung to the notion of an arbitrary God who might create or destroy at the drop of a hat—as in the story of Noah—or who occasionally needed to intervene to perform miracles in the lives of individuals. These theologians felt that determinism somehow infringed upon God's freedom to intervene in the world, and that determinism made for a self-directed universe which was entirely independent of God's governance.

Today, curiously, the anthropists take the same sort of position, arguing against the need for rationalizing the origin of the universe— but only in the name of accepting random probability as the creator. The ultimate reality, from their point of view, is that we are here, accidentally, and they therefore argue against the notion of any grand system of physical laws:

> The uncertainty principle had profound implications for the way in which we view the world. Even after more than fifty years they (these implications) have not been fully appreciated by many philosophers (such as myself), and are still the subject of much controversy. The uncertainty principle signaled an end to Laplace's dream of a theory of science, a model of the universe that would be completely deterministic: one certainly cannot predict future events exactly if one cannot even measure the present state of the universe precisely! We could still imagine that there is a set of laws that determines events completely for some supernatural being, who could observe the present state of the universe without disturbing it. However, such models of the universe are not of much interest to us ordinary mortals. It seems better to employ the principle of economy known as Occam's razor and cut out all the features of the theory that cannot be observed...[45]

To the anthropists, the fact that we cannot see God precludes us from affirming His existence. The problem with this line of reasoning, of course, is that it can be applied to any number of phenomena in our world that have never been observed, and which are—to some degree—controversial. However, the anthropists also pose a more serious and direct challenge to the existence of deity. Hawking ("A Brief History..." p. 122-123) asserts that quantum mechanics tends to refute the idea of a God-ordained Creation.[46] He notes that the universe would have been in a supremely chaotic state at the time of the big bang, and that *a Supreme Being would have been unlikely to use a framework of utter chaos as the basis for an "orderly" and "planned" creation*. He suggests that if a God truly created our universe, it is likely that He would have done so using orderly fundamental building blocks so that creation would manifest a very high degree of order, and so that Divine Order would be clearly evident from the tiniest levels of creation right up to the largest. Since the fundamental disorder of quantum mechanics (disorder from the perspective of the uncertainty principle) underlies all of creation, the anthropists assert that it is very unlikely that the universe was created by deity. Instead, they say, the fundamental disorder of the universe favors the parable of the typing monkeys and the notion of an accidental creation.

The arguments presented by the anthropists are almost, *but not quite*, compelling. Over the last few years, it has been strongly implied that quantum mechanics (and particle physics) does not, in fact, constitute the smallest and most fundamental level of creation. A relatively new theory instead ascribes order rather than disorder to the most fundamental realm of the universe. This theory, the "Theory of Heterotic Strings," effectively moves the most fundamental realm of creation down a notch, suggesting that particles are themselves composed of cosmic strings, and that at the level of these strings, the universe manifests great order and certainly not chaos. As we shall see in the next chapter, "String Theory" (as it is usually called) also provides something altogether unique and essential to the *God Theory*—a way to explain God's existence and nature, and His relationship to ourselves.

CHAPTER EIGHT

THE ETERNAL FRAMEWORK

Prior to general acceptance of the Big Bang Theory, theology was caught between a "steady-state" rock and a "Darwinist" hard place. An evolving, self-regulating universe without beginning or end, that automatically churned out life and perpetually maintained itself, seemed to have little overt need for a Divine Creator. After widespread acceptance of the Big Bang Theory, however, the steady-state vision of an infinite, eternal universe was effectively relegated to the scrap heap of bad scientific ideas. In Big Bang cosmology, the universe had a finite point-of-beginning—as in Genesis. And as in Genesis, the Big Bang Theory asserted that creation began with a flash of light. Next came matter, the forces of nature, indeed the current physical framework of the universe—almost exactly as provided in Genesis. *Suddenly the scientific version of creation seemed to parallel the Genesis version.* Suddenly, the world of science was surrounded by new circumstantial scientific evidence attesting to the possibility that the Bible was onto something. As the credibility of Genesis escalated, even skeptics had to face the very significant possibility that the Bible contained authentic Divine Revelation.

Though there is still much argument as to the credibility of scripture and the origin of the universe (as noted in the last chapter), it is clear that there is significant correlation between science and scripture, and this seems to greatly increase the likelihood that much of Genesis *is, in fact, an actual product of Divine Revelation.* The road from *"likelihood"* to *"certainty,"* however, is exceedingly long, arduous, and convoluted, requiring actual *proof* of the existence of a "Divine Creator." I will be the first to admit that *actual proof* of the existence of God remains beyond our capabilities. The basic problem is that science has never had anything remotely *scientific* upon which to base the existence of deity. Almost everyone concedes that belief in God is purely a matter of faith. Certainly, no one has ever distilled God in a chemistry laboratory. There are no photographs of Him, and we still can't call him up on the phone—despite television commercials to the contrary. The *God Theory*, may represent an attempt to provide a reasonable explanation of His existence, but because the theory is based, in part, on theological premises, it is not a platform designed to satisfy science. The theory's purpose is to dismantle archaic theology and spell out the need for a credible naturalistic theology predicated on science.

Today, metaphysics is still prominent in theology. Theologians explain God by saying that He is unexplainable. They sustain Him as Creator by asserting that He is omniscient and omnipotent; yet, they have no explanation for how He might have gained such great power and intelligence, and how He applies it. The best they can do is relate to biblical examples of how He used His power, and render us awestruck. They tell us that God is implicitly supernatural, or "above nature," that He is unexplainable in terms of natural forces, and that science has no adequate way in which to explain Him. But how is it that a being above and aloof from nature is able to relate to nature, to create, to regulate, and to destroy? Indeed, the very concept of a God who is literally "above nature," is nothing but "Ptolemaic" nonsense, bottling God into some imaginary sphere out beyond the limits of the "heavenly waters." We know that our universe just isn't made that way. There are no spheres. Any Grand Controller of nature would have to be a part of nature. To swim, He would be required to get His hands and feet wet.

Scripture tells us that God commanded the universe into being, in stages, but what do those commands represent and how did they work? Was it magical incantation, or a controlled thermodynamic alteration of the universe? How do we precisely explain it all, in scientific terms?

Answers to such questions depend upon our view of God—Who

and What He is, and where He is. Traditional explanations of God are timeworn and outdated, and treat Him as if He were a deity of incantation and magic. In the ancient world, magical incantation was a perfectly plausible explanation for creation. For that reason, and because of ancient Hebrew philosophy, God became a voice commanding us to "be" from some primordial who-knows-what. This view has only made God into a paradoxical wizard, wholly out-of-step with the rational, non-magical 21st Century. Every conclusion rendered by the *God Theory* refutes such treatment of The Almighty. Every rational quiver of the *God Theory* ultimately tells us that *God is a part of nature, and a natural outgrowth of the most fundamental building blocks of our universe.*

Before building the superstructure of a house, one must emplace solid footers and a good foundation. Before building new cells, the human body must first build a new framework of DNA/RNA and nutrients. Before building atoms, the universe had to churn out a vast array of electrons, protons and neutrons. Before the development of anything complex, in essence, a simple but solid infrastructure and/or supporting skeleton must exist. Everything that exists requires fundamental building blocks.

Physicists have long contended that the basis of the universe (its *forces* and *its matter*) is the simple particle. The Big Bang Theory tells us that all particles were created in the fires of the Big Bang, and therefore that all of the building blocks of our universe came into being in the same event. It is as if all of creation flowed outward from a single source. If that flow were on video tape, we might be able to reverse direction, run it backwards in slow motion, and witness everything merging into a single entity (providing we could eliminate the accompanying distortions of heat, fire and brilliance). At some definitive nanosecond in the creation process, moreover, it would be possible to show that all of the forces and material objects of nature were one. There were physical laws which governed that singular object, and those same laws continue to govern that which later exploded, split away and subdivided. Physicists have therefore reasoned for decades that physics should be unified, that there should be a *unified system of physical laws capable of describing every possible state of the universe, at any time, and every possible transitory state.*

Though *we* came into being long after **matter** and the *forces of nature* had gone their separate ways, it has been reasoned that there should be evidence in nature of these uniform physical laws, and that this evidence should show us how to re-integrate everything into a coherent whole. The problem is that we are still struggling to come to grips with basic laws of physics such as relativity and quantum mechanics. We are still debating whether the "Standard Model" is accurate, or not, whether the dichotomy of matter and antimatter (which is called symmetry) forms the basis of the physical universe, or whether the Standard Model should be replaced by a totally different model.

Though our state of knowledge is advanced in comparison to what it used to be, we are still *discovering*. The principles of modern physics have been slowly and painstakingly assembled over the past three thousand years. To paraphrase the words of Isaac Newton, modern physicists essentially stand upon the shoulders of giants. Physics would not exist without the likes of Pythagoras, Copernicus, Galileo, Huygens, Newton, Planck, Pauli, Heisenberg, and Einstein. While the laws of the universe have been pursued for thousands of years, all discoveries and contributions to those laws pale in the face of the explosion of knowledge that occurred during the 20th Century.

One of the greatest contributions of all times was the formulation of "*quantum mechanics*" by Max Planck, Louis de Broglie and others, in 1900. Quantum mechanics asserted that the universe is fundamentally composed of sub-atomic particles which provide the basis of all elements and compounds. Then, in 1905, Albert Einstein published his landmark "Special Theory of Relativity," which attempted to resolve longstanding problems in Newton's laws of motion. Special relativity asserted that the large objects of the universe are in constant motion, and that while all objects remain subject to uniform laws of nature, those laws may appear to vary based upon our perspective. The equation $E=MC^2$ was perhaps the most famous output of special relativity, describing a constant relationship between energy, matter and the speed of light. Special relativity was later validated with the explosion of the first atomic bomb. Ten years later, Einstein published his "General Theory of Relativity," which was devoted primarily to gravitation. It contained the notion that gravity might warp or bend three-dimensional space (and perhaps time) in the vicinity of large or very dense objects, and it contained mathematical theorems for predicting the effects of gravitational attraction.

By about 1965, quantum mechanics and relativity had matured into the giants of physics—quantum mechanics being concerned with the smallest units of matter and relativity the largest. At this point in time, four fundamental, discrete forces of nature were recognized: (1) the "*strong force*" binding the atomic nucleus together, (2) the "*weak force*" governing transformations of subatomic nuclei, (3) the "*electromagnetic force*" governing electricity, and (4) a poorly-understood phenomenon called "*gravity.*" By 1972, researchers had succeeded in unifying the electromagnetic and weak forces into a single "electroweak force." Then (Greenstein, "The Symbiotic Universe", p. 158):

> ...in 1974, the Harvard University physicists Howard Georgi and Sheldon Glashow took yet a further step and created a theory uniting the electroweak and strong forces. Three of the four fundamental forces of nature are encompassed in this grand unified theory, or GUT for short. Georgi and Glashow's work represents an immense generalization, breathtaking in its sweep, and it is one of the most important steps forward in the physics of our time. The grand unified theory gathers into one vast pattern the squeaking of chalk on a blackboard and the shining of the stars, radioactivity and the internal combustion engine, the compass needle and the nuclear reactor. Of all the phenomena of physics, only that of weight—gravity—is excluded from its

scope.[47]

Over the years, attempts to further unify physics have invariably uncovered two major problem-children: (1) the fundamental incongruency of quantum mechanics and relativity, and (2) gravity. Fitting quantum mechanics and relativity into a single theory seemed a virtual impossibility because the quantum mechanical laws that govern the smallest units of nature (i.e., particles) have little to do with the relativistic laws that govern the behavior of the largest units of nature (i.e. planets, stars and galaxies). Equally daunting was the process of shoe-horning gravity into particle theory, because all particles (real and virtual) seem to interact via *repulsion*. Gravity, on the other hand, is the sole force of nature that inter-relates objects in terms of their *attraction*.

There are, of course, many issues in physics that have never been completely answered. For example, Newton demonstrated that a prism can be used to break white light down into every spectral color, corresponding to differing wavelengths, seemingly proving that light is transmitted in waves rather than particles. Huygens' experiments had earlier sustained this notion, proving that light is propagated in waves like those produced when a stone is tossed into a pond. Much later, Maxwell and Hertz demonstrated that an accelerated charge can radiate electromagnetic waves into space, and that energy waves can augment, interfere with or even cancel each other out, depending entirely upon their frequency and wavelength. Such findings strongly validated Huygens' "Wave Theory of Light Propagation." However, Hertz later demonstrated that when a beam of light strikes a metal surface, electrons are ejected onto that surface. His findings effectively proved that *both particles and waves are involved in the transmission of light.* Thus, it became obvious that light had a *"dualistic nature,"* and that it behaved in a wavelike manner in addition to being carried along on individual particles known as photons.

Today, we still do not know the complete answer to this dilemma. How is it that light—a single phenomena—can be transmitted by both waves and particles? This so-called *"light enigma"* seems to suggest that the distinctions between waves and particles may be blurred at the most fundamental levels of nature. Support for this "blurring" also occurred in Einstein's Special Theory of Relativity. The simple formula $E=MC^2$ asserts that matter is convertible to energy, and vice-versa. Could matter effectively "unravel" to become energy, or energy "ball up" to become matter? Collectively, "special relativity" and the "light enigma" suggested that there might be a more basic mechanism than either particles or waves in the universe— that the universe might be composed of something common to both, but more basic than either. Many physicists believed that in order to effectively fit the laws of physics together into a unified whole, the light enigma and issues such as the incompatibility of quantum mechanics and relativity would have to be resolved. The latter problem was deemed particularly important. In the 1970s many physicists became dissatisfied with the so-called "Standard Model," predicated as it was on "particle physics." This model initially held that individual particles such as the photon and electron composed the universe. Later it was revised when such particles were, themselves, found to be composed of even smaller particles called "quarks." Dissatisfaction with the standard model eventually led to a totally new model of the universe based on *"String Theory."*

String Theory implicitly suggests: (1) that differences between matter and energy disappear at the very smallest and most fundamental levels of the universe, and (2) that both the *matter* and *forces* of nature arise due to the behavior of incomprehensibly tiny, "stringlike" filaments that compose everything. The precise nature of these tiny "strings" is still largely a matter of theoretical conjecture. One doesn't get too many definitive answers from books about string theory. Some physicists treat "strings" as if they were discrete, material filaments. Others suggest that they have no material substance at all, and that they are merely tiny energy wavelets, a sort of energy with structure.

More precisely, string theory asserts that particles are produced from fundamental *"loops"* in a *"string,"* and that these *loops*, in turn, *arise from patterns of interaction among strings.* As strings converge, diverge and otherwise interact, the theory holds that they *"vibrate."* Differing types/levels of interaction produce differing vibrations, which result in differing patterns of resonance (i.e. *"notes"*). *A certain type of note forms an electron; another a positron, a third a photon, etc.* The basic idea is that each type of particle is the result of a distinct type of note. Modern versions of string theory assert that matter and energy particles differ only in the types of "notes," resulting from various combinations of vibrations and fundamental "loops." The clear implication is that "strings" constitute the fundamental basis of all particles in the universe, and thus the most fundamental building blocks of our universe.

When initially formulated, string theory dealt only with the forces of nature and described how *"virtual particles"* which create the forces of the universe were formed. Such particles are collectively known as "bosons," and there are three different types: (1) the "photon" which carries the electroweak force, (2) the "gluon" which carries the strong nuclear force, and (3) the "graviton" which is thought to carry the gravitational force. The later application of string theory to the "real" particles of the material universe was, at first, questionable. Eventually, however, new ideas emerged suggesting that string interactions within a dense network might result in patterns of tension among various groups of strings. It was reasoned that this tension might then create fundamental notes and loops with de-facto substance, the result being real particles.

One must keep in mind that string theory is still very much "theory." The notion that strings might account for real as well as virtual particles (in addition to matter and antimatter) was called "symmetry." From symmetry, the idea of "Superstrings" emerged, and symmetry inferred that cosmic strings account for everything in the universe. Ultimately this was stated in the "Theory of Heterotic Strings," which also effectively incorporated the tenets of relativity as well as quantum mechanics. In this bold step, string theory became an all-encompassing Grand Unification Theory (or "GUT" for short), in which all physical laws and theories are inevitably synchronized.

The Theory of Heterotic Strings holds that cosmic "strings" exist in a microrealm, the "Planck Scale," which is the very smallest and most fundamental realm that can possibly exist in the universe:

> ...Strings are as small in comparison to a proton as a proton is in comparison to the solar system. This microrealm, named the Planck scale, is inaccessible to any conceivable experiment. Physicists and, increasingly, mathematicians, have nonetheless become entranced by the theory's rich structure. ("Particle Metaphysics" in Scientific American, February 1994, p. 97)[48]

The theory's "structure" is due to repetitive looping, constituting particles. While cosmic string structure is not totally predictable, it is orderly. It helps if we think of strings both individually, and in groups. A fundamental loop in an individual string might resemble a lasso in a cowboy's rope, but loops can also be formed by two superimposed U-shaped strings, one upright and the other upside-down. These differing types of loops would result in differing types of particles. It is possible, in essence, to think of strings individually or as "pairs," "triads," "sets," "groups," "complex groups," "group networks," and even "network systems." A single particle in space can be formed by a relatively simple loop involving one or just a few strings, but an object as big as the sun can only be described in terms of trillions of trillions of trillions of network systems of fundamental loops. The Milky Way galaxy, in turn, is the result of an unfathomable number of network systems. *In the penultimate, such string networks, whatever their density and complexity, span and fundamentally constitute—the entire universe. This is so because strings occur in association with any type of particle, be it virtual or real. Because gravity is an output of string theory, and because gravity has discernible and measurable effects across the whole of space, it is clear that cosmic strings span the void and are interlinked with each other, either directly or indirectly.* Moreover, the entire universe can be viewed as a complex mega-network of cosmic strings.

The notion of a "network-universe" is an inevitable by-product of the distribution of real and virtual particles throughout the cosmos. Real and virtual particles are well known to be everywhere, and if these particles are formed by simple and complex loops of cosmic strings, then one must conclude that cosmic strings are also everywhere and that a network of cosmic strings cris-crosses the fabric of space. Interestingly enough, this network-universe model is also sustained by theoretical efforts outside the realm of string theory. Abhay Ashtekar (and colleagues) of Syracuse Universe have found a way to re-write the equations of general relativity (relating to gravity) so that they resemble equations of quantum electrodynamics. The technique allows gravity to be treated as a quantum mechanical phenomenon, and avoids the mathematical problems that have plagued other attempts to synchronize relativity and quantum mechanics. Ashtekar's efforts imply that space is not just a seamless entity, but that it is instead composed of discrete infinitesimal loops and sheets of loops. Moreover, strings fundamental to particles, and particles fundamental to objects and forces compose every level of the universe that we can see. The inevitable result is not just a network, but an incredibly complex mega-network that directly or indirectly accounts for everything.

At the most complex levels, there are indescribably massive accumulations of cosmic strings tied up in colossal black holes. At the smallest and most fundamental levels are single stringlets and fundamental loops. The complexity of the underlying string network depends on the density of overlying objects in the superstructure of space. The network is always changing at the most complex levels of the universe, and it always remains complex. *At the very most fundamental level of the universe, however, there is nothing else.* The individual stringlet is the bottom tier of nature.

Strings can therefore be seen as the most fundamental of building blocks and the most basic of entities in the universe. They make up everything, but they themselves have no sub-components. ***Being physically the most fundamental of all units of the universe, they***

*are also the most original—which means that they inherently
existed before anything else.* This interesting notion, of course, runs
somewhat parallel to that expressed in the biblical notion of the
"originality of God." What is *"originality"*? It is a concept that can
be expressed either in *temporal terms*, or—perhaps more
appropriately in this case—in *physical terms.* In physical terms it
signals the most basic tier, the foundation that is necessarily emplaced
before any portion of the *superstructure*? In temporal terms, cosmic
strings are the most original of all the components of the universe,
because they inherently form the physical superstructure of all else,
and therefore nothing can exist without them.

Thus, we can recognize parallels between two concepts—the
"originality of cosmic strings," and the "originality of God," the latter
of which is a theological doctrine based upon Genesis 1:1, asserting
that God existed before anything else. Might these two concepts
somehow fit together? I think so! Let's go directly to the punch line—
the *God Theory* asserts that they are a perfect fit, that "Heterotic
strings" and "Almighty God" are essentially one and the same, and
that *"God," in fact, is a living, thinking, energy-being resulting
from the existence of a network of cosmic strings that spans the
entire universe.* How so? The answer is very simple. *Just as the
human persona comes into being as a product of the
interconnection of stringlike neurons within the human brain, so
God comes into being as a product of the interconnection of cosmic
strings across the universe.* This being the case, God is a natural
outgrowth of the universe, and the universe is a natural
outgrowth of God. Taking the foregoing analogy one-step farther,
we note that the persona of the human body is seated in the head,
though neurons extend downward into the arms and legs as well
as the brain, the effect being the ability of the brain to relate to
and regulate the fingers, the toes and all in-between. Though the
brain is separate from the fingers and toes, it is also, in an
important sense, an integral part of them. The *God Theory* applies
the same general notion to God. It asserts that the persona of
God lies at the "God Point" (which will be defined just a bit

later) but that His (de-facto neural) connections span the entire universe, the result being His ability to relate uniformly to the Earth, the "Big Dipper," the "Great Attractor," an individual atom, a bug, or the very tiniest of sub-atomic particles. Man is in the image of God in the sense that His mind and persona, i.e. his being, is formed and composed of interconnections. We cannot view individual neural connections in the human brain and discern the associated human personality. The personality comes from the interaction of those neurons. It is the same with God. But where neurons are physical structures that interact via discrete electrical pulses, cosmic strings are more like momentary lines of force (as in a lightning bolt) that are not bound by the speed limitations of special relativity since they are innately "virtual," and lack mass. The effect is virtually instantaneous communication across vast portions of the universe. The entire universe becomes a facet of God's neural network and a component of His being, and His being and intellect is effectively dispersed across the network. He becomes accessible from all parts of the universe, simultaneously.

The Bible regards God as a spirit, but a spirit can also be seen as a "virtual" or "energy-being" (there is really no difference). Cosmic strings playing the notes of virtual particles, and composing the neural-network of the God of scripture are thus seen to assemble and compose a Being whose essence is that of immense, intelligent energy, and Who is not altogether bound by the familiar laws of this universe. We therefore arrive at a coherent explanation of the scriptural incidents in which God variously appears as a pillar of fire, a burning bush, an image with the likeness of fire, a bright and shining entity upon Whom no one could gaze and live, etc.

Is it not logical that a virtual being, an energy-being with intelligence, a deity intimately interconnected to the entire universe (and all of its forces) might have immense reserves of power at his/her fingertips? As the human persona exercises neural connectivity and control over the human body, so the Divine Persona exercises neuro-virtual interconnective control across the entire universe. Being unlimited in expanse, He is unlimited in power. Being interconnected to all particles, virtual and real, He can implicitly feed upon all of the available power of the universe. Those same interconnections allow Him a de-facto "omnipresence" and "omniscience" as well as "omnipotence." He becomes not only The Supreme Power, but also The Supreme Intelligence.

Werner Von Braun has been quoted as observing that after a scientist has spent decades studying the universe, he inevitably begins to feel that there is something back there, hidden, beyond what you can see and feel and hear with the natural senses...[49] This something is a living, thinking, interactive being and a force, almost in the Star Wars sense; but also a being with a focus and a morality Who is alert, vibrant, purposeful, and in no way mystical. The energy being and force that is the God of our universe is integral to every flash of electricity, every particle, every wisp of smoke, every human cell, every planet, every sun, every galaxy, the largest, the smallest, all that has ever existed, and all that will ever exist! From this, another major premise of the *God Theory* arises; it simply asserts what we have already said—that God is integral to and a natural outgrowth of the universe, and that His essence is that of a network of cosmic strings spanning the entire universe, a network forming interconnections that make everything a part of The One, and The One a part of everything.

So, where does this take us? Let's synthesize a bit more. The following are important premises of the *God Theory*: (1) the universe is closed and oscillating, by Divine Plan; (2) the pattern for the universe was pre-ordained and established in the mix of matter and energy in the Big Bang; (3) there are two scriptures, the written word and the physical creation—study of the natural world can point to scriptural truths, and this establishes the principle of "scriptural dynamism"; (4) gravity caused the physical evolution of our universe and is a manifestation of The Almighty, (5) God is a pantheistic virtual being, and (6) the entire universe is interconnected by cosmic strings.

What I find most exciting about the *God Theory* is the fact that it can be sustained by real, physical evidence. The "force of gravity" is direct evidence in support of the existence of a pan-universal network of cosmic strings. The force of gravity, in turn, is almost entirely responsible for the physical structure of the universe, and the evolution of life. Its significance is so overwhelming that it can be likened to the "Hand of God, in motion."

We know that gravity exists because we can see that objects are gravitationally attracted to each other across the whole of intergalactic space, and we can measure those effects. But gravity is also a very difficult concept to deal with, scientifically. Particle physics does not rationally explain how objects can attract each other across the immense distances of space. The binary stars of Alpha Centauri and our own sun, for example, exert mutual attraction and affect each other's movements, though only slightly, across a distance of four light years. Mutual attraction between two objects at such a distance seems intuitively impossible unless they are somehow interconnected. This, of course, provides some of the strongest intuitive rationale in support of string theory, suggesting that the entire universe is interconnected. Gravity is the only force that is attractive, while all others are repulsive.

Quantum theory tells us that all the FORCES of nature are produced by "VIRTUAL PARTICLES," and that gravity, the first of the great forces of nature to emerge after the Big Bang, is a product of a "VIRTUAL" particle called the "graviton." One cannot hope to understand virtual particles, unless one also has an understanding of REAL PARTICLES. Matter is formed from "real particles," and real particles are distinguished by the fact that they: (1) have mass, and (2) obey an essential law of quantum mechanics called the "Pauli Exclusion Principle," which asserts that no two particles of matter can simultaneously occupy the same precise point in space. The Pauli Exclusion Principle tells us that real particles take up space, and that as a product of this they can interact and collide with other real particles. Collision, in turn, can cause them either to self-destruct in bursts of energy, or perhaps instead coalesce with other particles, break apart, bounce around and/or take new positions in space. In the process of doing one of these things they almost always directly alter the composition and chemistry of the universe. Real particles can be discerned by a device called a particle detector, which is designed to deflect photons off particles with substance and sense the return from the impact. Virtual particles cannot be detected by this method because they lack substance.

Unlike real particles, virtual particles take up NO space, and nothing therefore precludes any two (or more) of them from occupying the same point in space. Neither does their presence or absence DIRECTLY alter the sub-atomic composition and chemistry of the universe. Since they convey forces, however, their presence can very significantly alter the energy-state of real particles (matter), indirectly imposing changes on the composition and chemistry of the universe.

A property called "spin" is very useful in distinguishing between real and virtual particles. "Spin" tells how particles look and behave during movement. For example, a particle of spin "0" (low energy state) looks like a dot and exhibits the same appearance from every direction. A particle of spin "1," on the other hand, is like an arrow—it changes appearance when moved but resumes its original appearance after it has been turned through one complete revolution. A particle of spin "2" is such that it resumes its original appearance after one-half of a complete revolution (after 180 degrees). *All particles of spin 0, 1 or 2 are, by definition, "virtual."* All Particles of mass (real particles), by contrast, have a spin of only 1/2, which means that they resume their original shape after spinning through two complete revolutions. Real and virtual particles are also distinguished by their mode of interaction, as described in the following:

> In quantum mechanics, the FORCES or interactions BETWEEN matter particles are all supposed to be carried by particles of integer spin—0, 1, or 2. What happens is that a matter particle, such as an electron or a quark, emits a force-carrying particle. The recoil from

this emission changes the velocity of the matter particle. The force-carrying particle then collides with another matter particle and is absorbed. This collision changes the velocity of the second particle, just as if there had been a force between the two matter particles.[50]

Unification of the strong nuclear, weak nuclear and electromagnetic forces showed that all three forces stem from a single virtual particle, that a transition from one type of force to another occurs as this single particle becomes increasingly energetic. "Electromagnetism" is produced by "photons," which occur at low to moderate energy levels. At somewhat higher energy levels photons become "massive vector bosons, which produce the "weak nuclear force." At still higher energy levels bosons become "gluons" and produce the "strong nuclear force." Moreover, THREE of the FOUR major forces of nature are produced by a virtual particle of spin 1. Quantum theory says that the fourth force, gravity, is produced by a virtual particle called a "graviton," which has "spin 2." Gravity is thus distinguished from the other forces of nature (in quantum theory) by the unique spin of the graviton, and gravitons are thought to be exchanged incessantly by particles of spin 1/2 ("real particles"). Curiously, however, no such exchange has ever been observed.

Gravitational experiments show only: (1) that gravity is omnipresent, expressed throughout the universe, and always attractive, (2) that gravity is normally the weakest of the forces of nature, and (3) that under certain conditions gravity can become the strongest of the natural forces. While the gravitational attraction between two very small objects at considerable distance is minuscule; a supermassive black hole may become gravitationally potent enough to devour an entire galaxy, or perhaps even entire galaxy-*clusters*. Though its power increases or decreases as a function of distance, no one can dispute the fact that the force of gravity is omnipresent and clearly manifested. The Moon orbits the Earth, the Earth orbits the Sun, the Sun orbits a black hole at the center of the Milky Way Galaxy, and the Milky Way Galaxy is one of a cluster of galaxies held in relative place and being drawn into the Great Attractor. The Great Attractor, in turn, is being drawn toward something with unfathomable mass lying hundreds of millions or perhaps even billions of light years out in space. What lies beyond this colossal "granddaddy" of the Great Attractor can only be a matter for speculation, but something assuredly does, that assuredly has spectacular gravitational power.

What we can see from all this is that as the gravitational power of an object increases, its power over and effect upon the objects of a surrounding area rapidly escalates. In a string theoretic sense, a gravitationally powerful object has more interconnections with objects in a surrounding orb than a smaller object. In the end, the greatest gravitational power and the greatest connectivity is always clearly manifested at the weighted center of an array of objects. The power of whatever occupies the gravitationally-weighted center is simultaneously felt throughout the entire array.

If the "array" happens to be the entire universe, the interconnections of the object occupying the weighted gravitational center necessarily extend throughout the universe. This is a very important point. It means that every object, every particle, *every string* is tied directly or indirectly to the center. Attraction exists throughout the network in direct proportion to the distribution of interconnections about the network, creating "tension" and the force of gravity, but also a "network-universe" that is intimately tied together. Gravitational focal points within that network result from the "bunching" and the "density of bunching" of the network. Whatever lies at the center is the most "bunched" and "interconnected" of all, and is thus in control of the entire show. When we apply string theory in this manner, we can neatly and comprehensively explain how gravity works, why it is always attractive rather than repulsive, and why the entire universe is necessarily interconnected. The distribution of known gravitational forces about the universe, and their measured power, sustain this notion—as objects increase in size and gravitational power, they control an increasingly large array of objects.

In the end, it is certain that our own Moon, Earth and Sun are gravitationally tied, indirectly, to the Great Attractor and its "Granddaddy," and ultimately, through a succession of even larger objects, to a colossal black hole, or perhaps a cluster of supermassive black holes, occupying the true gravitational center of the universe. All of these objects, in succession, gravitationally attract my fingers as they type these words, and your hand as you work your way through the pages of this book. Their gravitational clout ultimately impacts the entire universe. Because we can see and feel and measure the effect of colossal black holes like the "Great Attractor's Grandad," we can be certain that the entire universe is intimately tied together by an unseen force called gravity. This being the case, the universe would certainly seem to be "tied" together by cosmic strings, because objects can only attract one another across the vast distances of interstellar space if they are somehow linked. Standard particle theory does not adequately explain attractions across immense distances. And because no "graviton" has ever been detected by any means after nearly a century of investigation, many physicists believe that it is high time to move on to something else. It should be noted that the "Standard Model" has had many other problems, not the least of which is a requirement that the number of particles of matter and antimatter in the early universe approximate each other. Studies are increasingly suggesting that this could not have been possible given the scarcity of antimatter now, which is taken by many physicists as just another of many strong indications that it is time to move on to something else—that something, of course, being string theory.

String theory not only resolves the dilemmas of particle physics, it unifies relativity and quantum mechanics, and duplicates their projections. Einstein's General Theory of Relativity was primarily concerned with gravitation, and the so-called "gravity model" is an important contribution of physics to engineering, transportation planning, finance and marketing (among other activities). It has been found that models based on the "Theory of Heterotic Strings" can also predict the impact of gravity, and that such models can substantially duplicate the outputs of the gravity model and general relativity.

String theory has the potential power to allow us to define the precise gravitational center of the universe. Simultaneously, it tells us that this point will have the best connections to all other points, and that it will have the maximum gravitational power in the universe. At the same time, this point (object) would be the ultimate focal point of vibrations of notes played by the pan-universal cosmic string network. Its centrality would make it the recipient of all de-facto communications occurring within that network. **Having the maximum possible interaction potential with the remainder of the universe, it can appropriately be thought of as the "God Point"—the point at which the mind and being of a pantheistic living entity might have arisen due to constant stimulation and interaction across a pan-universal network of Heterotic strings.**

Being both the communications centerpoint and gravitational centerpoint of the universe, the God Point, remarkably, is also necessarily the point from which the Big Bang did its thing. So, the entire universe can be traced to the God Point. The power of the Big Bang eminated from this point, and so did the force of gravity, which became the primary shaping and controlling force in the universe. From the God Point, in other words, came gravity, the creative "Hand of God," which reached out and gave the universe form and substance—particles, the forces of nature, chemistry, physical evolution, the galaxies, our solar system, our world and ecosystem, and finally ourselves.

As the God Point was the center of creation, so shall it also be the center of destruction and cataclysm. Gravity will someday grow strong enough to cause the universe to close and collapse upon itself and to be consumed in heat and fire as it does so. The scriptures boldly speak of a "*lake of fire*," sealing the fate of all that is imperfect, and making ready for a new round of creation—a new universe in which righteousness shall prevail. As The Almighty created forces which hurled the galaxies into place, it seems that a time will come when He will gather them back into the "potters furnace." And after that moment, perhaps the Alpha shall once again spring from the

Omega, and the wonderful scriptural promise of a "new heaven and a new Earth" shall be fulfilled.

CHAPTER NINE

THE THEORY AND THE FUTURE:
WHERE WE GO FROM HERE

The central message of this book is that "God" is a credible concept. Everything can be traced to the "God Point" via scientific reasoning, and string theory seems to explain the existence and fundamental nature of God. At the same time, striking correlation between science and scripture suggests that God has revealed Himself to us. *The God Theory*, moreover, poses a frontal assault on the age-old notion that science cannot explain, or perhaps even prove, the existence of God. A tremendous amount of scientific information has been linked to scripture in this book, justifying belief in an Omnipotent Creator. However, to promote "readability" only a broad summary of that information has been presented. No single book can deal with *all* or even *most* of the scientific and theological issues about God and remain coherent—and transportable. (Had this book emphasized evolution, for example, it could easily have been two or three times its current size, and analysis of Darwinism would certainly have distracted from the primary theme of Who and What God really is.)

While a number of conclusions have been made about the nature of God and eternity, it should be noted that the findings of *The God Theory* do not exclusively rule out, or in, either the Hindu-Buddhist view of eternity, or the Judeo-Christian-Islamic view. Many questions remain. Even if the universe is closed and oscillating, and even if the notion of a closed universe is consistent with the notion of a biblical doomsday, what lies beyond that doomsday with regard to the individual (and the individual soul) is still at issue. A Buddhist might contend that the "next life" will simply occur in the new creation on the far side of the omega-state universe—rather than here in this universe—and thereby sustain the notion of reincarnation and a chain of existence. While *The God Theory* unfolds from the Judeo-Christian-Islamic point of view, it cannot ultimately rule out the Hindu-Buddhist view of eternity. The notion of a closed, oscillating universe can be shoehorned, it seems, into either perspective.

Nevertheless, the findings do appear to confirm many things that are, more or less, biblical—such as the "light correlation," the sequence of creation, the notion of truth, the "lake of fire," the new creation. I am also increasingly fascinated by the words of Jesus appearing in the Gospel of Thomas suggesting that God is pantheistic and conterminous with nature. The findings of *The God Theory* clearly support such a viewpoint, and suggest that the Gospel of Thomas may be worthy of additional study.

The findings of *The God Theory* also suggest that the message of "young Earth creationists" is outdated and unsuitable for the 21st Century and the new millennium. Literalistic belief in a 24-hour creation day is unsupportable by either science or scripture, and seems to undercut belief in deity. The time has clearly come to dismantle archaic theology and build a new theological foundation steeped in science and wholly appropriate for future millennia.

I have come to believe that God made Himself known to humanity many times in the distant past, to many different peoples, and through many different religions, but that humanity—as often as not—has compromised His message due to a prevailing lack of knowledge. The scientific and philosophical preconditions for understanding the nature of God (and Creation) would not be established until the 20th Century. The human relationship to God in the 10th Century B.C. could only incorporate awe and reverence, as well as superstition, magic, myth, and bad science. As a result, God's contacts and instructions were always subject to human "double-distillation" and were always retrofitted with tons of cultural baggage. The great human quest is, and has always been, the preservation of the status quo, and in this quest new ideas are regularly and routinely remolded to fit popular preconceptions. As a result, archaic and distorted views of the Divine have been sustained and promulgated, and these have sometimes been passed down via political and ecumenical machinery to become laws that were impossible to resist. Indeed, prevailing views of the First and Second Centuries, A.D. remain enmeshed in today's religious doctrines, traditions, and even ritual. If we retain them because they remind us of the wonderful times when the prophets, the messiah and/or the apostles walked the Earth, that's one thing, but if we see such archaic views as utter truth, then we're guilty of self-deception. Scientific findings are continually undercutting archaic views of God and creation, and continuing theological support for such views is slowly-but-surely driving people away from their religious roots. The handwriting is on the wall. If Judeo-Christian-Islamic tenets are to survive, mainline views about God, eternity and the universe must be reshaped.

At the same time, I will be the first to admit that it is possible to have an incorrect view of God and eternity while maintaining a strong personal relationship with The Divine, in the Calvinist sense. For this reason, it has never been my purpose to portray biblical literalists and fundamentalists as evil or worthy of ostracism. "Calvinist" principles have provided Christians with powerful rationale for high moral standards and close personal ties to The Almighty. Nothing is wrong with this. Furthermore, all of history shores up Calvin's assertion that God's chief goal is and will remain the cultivation of a close and enduring relationship with His Creation. God's main problem is that much of His creation has a mind of its own. Humanity, in order to survive, has had to respond to the environment and develop its own survival techniques and social standards. These have always included superstition as well as secular traditions founded in ignorance, and to say that these have not impacted religion is the height of naiveté. Today, voices of an archaic past are very much alive in our religious activities, including a preference for the mystical and an inability to connect with the "naturalism" that is altogether implicit in the words of Psalms 19:1: "The heavens declare the glory of God and the firmament showeth His handiwork."

Driven by the "Great Commission" of Christ to evangelize all nations, many Christian leaders have long since lost their focus on the necessity of also evangelizing the world with a "coherent theology" that will be truly appropriate for the new millennia—and which will not continue to drive educated people away from the tenets of religion. There can be no coherent new theology, however, if theologians disregard the obvious and proven ties between nature and scripture. God did not create a world and a universe and then turn around and deny the essence of that creation in His scriptural revelation. His "written" and His "created" messages are one, and any theological position to the contrary is a product of human "double distillation" and error. The heavens are the handwriting of God, and they deserve *at least* the same respect as the written word.

The key to building an appropriate new theology for the new millennium is open-mindedness, and respect for science. Many denominations have wrapped themselves in fundamentalism and built around themselves an impenetrable barrier of tradition and sacrosanct beliefs. Others recognize that the flowering of scriptural truths is a continual process and seem to remain open to theological innovation. There are three basic views on how to interface with Genesis: (1) "Young Earth Creationism," (2) "Old Earth Creationism," and (3) "Theistic Evolution." In the future, every denomination and religious group will have to choose from among these three very divergent ideals. *Young Earth Creationism* obviously stems from a traditional, literalistic interpretation of Genesis, which this book has soundly rejected. There are three broad lines of evidence against this notion: (1) scientific arguments proving that an "instantaneous" six-day creation simply did not happen, (2) scriptural evidence suggesting that portions of Genesis have been heavily edited and revised, and (3) portions of scripture suggesting that the term "day" refers to a generalized "sphere of time" rather than a distinct 24-hour day.

Many biblical scholars question the authority of portions of the First Chapter of Genesis because of prosaic and historical evidence suggesting editing and recomposition. As noted in the introductory chapters, the captive Hebrew Priests of Babylon conducted the last known editing of Genesis about 560 B.C., wherein they introduced the notions of a six-day creation and a Sabbath Day for resting and giving thanks to God. Their efforts were designed to assemble the Jewish people in the synagogues on the Sabbath and instill in them the customs and religious teachings necessary to preserve the national identity. Fear was at the basis of their efforts—fear of outright assimilation into greater Babylon.

Unfortunately, no one can say with absolute precision what the original "Yahwist" Genesis was like. The Second Chapter of Genesis, however, provides a likely pattern of prose and verbiage, and suggests that anything contributed by the Yahwists to what we now recognize as the First Chapter of Genesis would have been set in a *timeless* context. If Chapter One was only "revised," in succession, by the Elohists, Deuteronomists, and Hebrew Priests of Babylon, and if it was "originally authored" by the Yahwists, the original version *might* have looked something like the following:

1. In the beginning, God created the heavens and the earth.

2. And the Earth was without form and void, and darkness was upon the face of the deep, and the Spirit of God moved upon the face of the waters.

3. And God said, "Let there be light!" And there was light.

4. And God saw the light that it was good, and God divided the light from the darkness.

5. The light He called day, and the darkness He called night.

6. And in the day that the Lord God made the earth and the heavens, He set two great lights in the heavens, the greater to rule the day, and the lesser to rule the night...."

7. And the Lord God set a dividing line in the heavens separating the waters of creation from the waters of the deep.

8. And then commanded He the waters of creation to

be gathered together into one place to form the world.
9. And when the world had been formed, He
commanded the solid places to appear.
10. And in that day, the Lord God gathered the waters
of the Earth together into one place, calling them "seas,"
and in like manner He gathered the dry ground together,
calling it "land."
11. And the Lord God commanded the land to produce
vegetation: seed-bearing plants and trees, and fruit with
seed in it, according to their various kinds.
12. And after that the land produced vegetation: plants
bearing seed and trees bearing fruit with seed in it, each
according to their kinds.
13. And in the day of Creation, the Lord God recognized
the beauty and grandeur of all that He had created.
14. And within that Creation the Lord God had provided
order, with the heavens and the heavenly bodies
reflecting the passage of time, the separation of day
from night, the separation of years into seasons.
15. And all that was created was of a design that would
benefit the Earth.
16. And within that design was a greater light which
the Lord God had created to rule the day, and a lesser
light to rule the night. These and the stars, also, were
designed by the Lord God to give light upon the Earth.
17. And all Creation was of a design to give light, beauty
and order to the Earth.
18. And God saw that everything was good.
19. And in that day the Lord God also commanded the
waters of the Earth to teem with living animals.
20. Also placed He living creatures, birds to fly across
the expanse of the sky above the waters.
21. And so it was that God created the great creatures
of the sea and every living and moving thing of the sea,
according to their kind, and every winged bird of the

air according to its kind. And God saw that it was good.

22. And God blessed these creatures, saying: "Be fruitful and increase in numbers, filling the waters of the seas and all that is above the seas.

23. And in that day the Lord God commanded the dry land to produce all kinds of living animals, each according to their kind, and it was so.

24. And among these were wild animals, livestock, and the lowly creatures that move along the ground, each after their own kind.

25. Then God said, "Let us make man in our own image, who shall be appointed to rule over the fish of the sea and the birds of the air, the livestock, and over all the earth, and even the lowly creatures that move along the ground."

26. So God made man in His own image, in the image of God He created him; male and female He created them.

27. And God blessed them and said: "Be fruitful and multiply, and fill the earth and subdue it. Rule over the fish of the sea and the birds of the air and over every living creature that moves upon the ground."

28. Then God said, "I give to you every seed-bearing plant on the face of the whole earth and every tree that has fruit with seed in it. They will be yours for food.

29. And to all the beasts of the earth and all the birds of the air and all the creatures that move on the ground—everything that has the breath of life in it—I give the green plants for their food." And it was so.

30. And the Lord God saw all that He had made, that it was exceedingly good.

Genesis 2:

1. Thus the heavens and the earth were completed in

all their vast array.

2. And having completed Creation, the Lord God ceased His labors, and set aside a time of rejoicing and celebrating the creation.

3. And He commanded that man should do the same, that man should cease his labors, remember, honor and celebrate the Lord for the great works of Creation.

I offer this only as an example of what the original Yahwist version of the first portion of Genesis might have been like. The foregoing is purely speculative, and it is not my intent that it should ever become a portion of any scriptural interpretation. Importantly, this example shows that removing specific timeframes (and re-establishing the unmistakable Yahwist tone that appears in the Second Chapter of Genesis) does nothing innately harmful to the scriptures. Instead, what comes to the fore is a perpetuation of a very old and beautiful message—that the Lord God created the universe, and that the events of creation were special and exceedingly marvelous—altogether deserving of commemoration. Should our descendants someday nail down the errors of past editing and/or more precisely pin down an expanded Yahwist creation account, God will lose nothing in the way of credit, and He may, in fact, gain much in the way of credibility.

While "Young Earth Creationists," hold to the notion that the Earth was created in six literal, 24-hour days, and that it is perhaps only about five thousand years old, "*Old Earth Creationists*" believe that God intimately guided the creation process across countless millennia and distinct stages of creation to arrive at the universe in its present form. They diverge sharply with *Young Earth Creationists* by asserting that the universe was created in six distinct "*phases*" rather than six distinct "*24-hour days*." The following is a persuasive description of the ***biblical*** evidence supporting Old Earth Creationism:

At first reading the creation account seems to indicate

that these six days of creative activity were twenty-four hours each... the question is not in what time God *could* create the world, but in what time periods God in fact *did* create all the basic kinds of things in existence.

Further examination of Scripture indicates that the term "day" does not always designate twenty-four hours. The Hebrew term for "day" (Yom) can denote (1) the period of light in contrast to the period of darkness, (2) a period of twenty-four hours, (3) a point of time, (4) a year, or (5) a long "time." "Day" meant a month (Gen. 29:14), seven Sabbaths of years (Lev. 25:8), "a long time" (forty years) in the desert (Josh. 24:7), and another "long time" when Israel was without the true God (2 Chron. 15:3).

In the context of (the traditional) Genesis I the solar system was not arranged to regulate days and nights until the fourth day, and then the "day" was not twenty-four hours, but the period of light in contrast to the darkness of the night (Gen. 1:18)... A period of time longer than twenty-four hours is also indicated between the creation of Adam and of Eve. But before Eve was created, Adam's initial excitement with his new vocation of caring for the garden subsided long enough for him to become lonely (2:15, 18). And enough time then had to pass for all the kinds of animals and birds God created to pass before him for classifying and naming (2:19-20).

Although references to the "evening" and the "morning" on each of the creation days (Gen. 1) has seemed to many to indicate twenty-four hour days, the literal meaning is not invariable even after the fourth day... clearly figurative uses for longer periods of time do, in fact, occur. "The brevity of human life is like that of grass, for in the morning it springs up new, by evening it is dry and withered" (Ps 90:5-6). As the original Schofield Bible note on Genesis 1:5 explained, "The use of evening and morning may be held to limit "day" to the solar day; but the frequent parabolic use of natural phenomena may warrant the conclusion that each creative "day" was a period of time marked off by a beginning and ending.[51]

In the desert during their flight across the Sinai from Egypt, God gave the Israelites "meat in the evening, and in the morning bread to the full." Mornings and evenings became special times celebrating birth (or rebirth) and death, and the eternal presence of God. Passover celebrations begin during the evening and last until sundown of the following day. Evenings and mornings are also seen as times for reverence, prayer, and thanksgiving to God. As used in the First Chapter of Genesis, the terms "evening" and "morning" become commemorative celebrations of the start and completion of an act of God. The same is true with the delivery of manna and meat to the Hebrews in the Wilderness. Using strict literalism as their guide, "Young Earth Creationists" have drawn these elements of Hebrew tradition out of context. Careful study of Genesis, itself, tells us that the Sixth Day, the day of creation of Adam and Eve, actually encompassed many days. A thorough analysis of scripture (in addition to science) ultimately indicates that the ultra-literalists are all wet.

"*Old Earth Creationism*," on the other hand, is easily supported by both science and scripture, and is a concept providing for extensive scientific-scriptural harmony. Because its thesis is fully capable of embracing an Earth billions of years in age, science cannot disavow it. Also, I personally cannot disavow Old Earth Creationism because I cannot disavow the possibility that God might have intimately guided creation from Point A through Point Z. However, Old Earth Creationism is weakened, in my opinion, by its literalistic roots, and by the compendium of scientific evidence which intimately links life to processes of organic and inorganic evolution. Furthermore (*and most importantly*), it seems to me that the entire concept of a "creation day" is now suspect because of: (1) scriptural editing by those of the "Priestly Perspective," during the Babylonian captivity, and (2) the essentially timeless message of Genesis, Chapter Two, which conflicts with that of Chapter One, and must be considered authoritative because it was written 500 years earlier. Indeed, the available evidence suggests that the Yahwists did not intend to associate a specific time period with the events of creation! While both the phrase "...in that day..." and the term "day," are both used in Chapter Two, these terms *always* carry a loose and utterly timeless meaning. *The Yahwist message eloquently sustains a notion that creation was continual and undivided,* that it can be thought of as a single action spanning a generalized timeframe—the length of which is not specified. This notion of a single creative action is most consistent with a doctrine of "Theistic Evolution."

Those who revised Genesis, in Babylon, may have done so under the inspiration of an Almighty *who clearly wanted to save the Nation of Judah*, but the effected scriptural changes seem to have introduced error (i.e. "Young Earth Creationism), and a propensity for misinterpretation because of the division of the events of creation into questionable time phases. In the sense that both versions of "creationism," divide the events of creation into distinct time periods and therefore promote misinterpretation, both ideas would seem to deny the fundamental "truth premise" that stems from both Deuteronomy and science. Either the Hebrew Priests of Babylon erred in what they did, or the Bible presents us with an example of Divine Guidance that leads inevitably to paradox. A real divinity would not lead us into the realm of paradox; only men would do that.

While the revisions of the Priestly Perspective preserved the Hebrew Nation so that the Jewish people might be able to fulfill the greater promises and prophecies of scripture, an inescapable result of those efforts is the deep theological dilemma that we currently find ourselves in—a dilemma that promotes atheism and agnosticism on the one hand, and religious fanaticism and theological error on the other. How can a perfect God have authored something of this nature?

Alternatives for dealing with this dilemma include: (1) returning the scriptures to their original Yahwist format, which is an impossibility, (2) inserting much more detail into translations like the "Living Bible" to ensure that the scriptures are interpreted in their proper historical, cultural, geo-political and scientific format, (3) heavily footnoting passages of known and suspected editing, or (4) simply ignoring the situation. In reality, there is no satisfactory answer to this problem.

Correlation of the Yahwist scriptures with science inevitably links The Divine realm to the natural, and further validates the notion of *Theistic Evolution*. Theistic Evolution is overwhelmingly sustained by the logic of this book, which upholds the thesis *that God created via explainable processes, and not magic*. Available evidence suggests that God stacked the cards of creation to achieve most if not all of His creative goals via a single event—the Big Bang. Whether He intervened in and fine-tuned various creation phases and processes from time-to-time is a matter for endless and altogether meaningless debate. *Evolution, in my opinion, is simply the way He did it. It was God's "creation process."* Only evolution is sustained by the scientific and scriptural doctrines of truth as well as scriptural dynamism. Theistic Evolution does not rob God of His grandeur. Like its competing notions, it asserts that the universe is the product of a Divine Plan, and that God is ultimately the Creator and sustainer of all things. This is, however, a different mode of interaction between God and Creation, wherein the method of creation becomes somewhat analogous to that of software engineer tailoring a program to meet certain goals, and then fine-tuning the results through the installation process.

Biblical ultra-literalism obscures the power, majesty, and complexity, of such a creation process, and simultaneously transforms God into a mysterious shaman, of sorts, Who simply "poofs" things into being. At the same time, it obscures profound and profoundly hidden messages of Genesis. The best example of this is provided by *earlier observations relating to Genesis 1:2, and the phrase "...darkness was upon the face of the deep." In English, there is* *only one word for "darkness." In ancient Hebrew, however, there were two distinct words—"aphela" which was used to denote the absence of light, as in English, and "khoshekh" which was used to denote a state of darkness that had its own unique **physical properties**. The **striking, and thrilling parallels** between the modern notion of a "black hole" and the Hebrew "khoshekh" are completely obscured by literalism. Similarly, literalism precludes proper interpretation of the story of Ruth, which is really a protest against tyranny. The only thing that literalism really promotes is the interpretation of the bible by commonfolk and those of lesser education. At the same time, it leaves the innate"holes of scripture" unplugged, and all-too-easy to fill with the imagination of fundamentalist preachers, and others.* Literalism does not provide a way out of the dilemma that we find ourselves in; it only deepens the hole that we are struggling to climb out of.

Scriptural dynamism does not preclude appropriate applications of literalism, it simply emphasizes the need to establish proper scientific, historical and cultural context in interpretations and doctrines. It is simply the best way to deal with the host of modern theological issues that confront and threaten to overwhelm us. *The God Theory* tells us that God is real, it explains His existence, and effectively deals with a broad range of theological issues and problems. Ultimately, it sustains many of the assertions of rationalism and naturalism while linking such ideas to scripture, and illustrating the power of scientific-scriptural *composites* in explaining the greater mysteries of the universe.

Ours is an age of theological retrenchment and religious conservatism, in which theologians storm at us from the pulpit with "eternal and unyielding truths of scripture." However, if we but *go back* to the time of John Calvin and Isaac Newton, to a more progressive era in many ways, we find that there was widespread belief in the notion that science unfolds scriptural truths, and that the unfolding of scriptural truths is a continuous process. The blunt truth is that we lost this perspective in the fiery debates that followed the advent of Darwinism. It has taken hundreds of years for some of us to come to a realization that *Theistic Evolution* points to the Almighty with no less fervor than creationism, and perhaps even more! Perhaps it was this realization that recently led the Roman Catholic Church (under the leadership of Pope John Paul II) to make positive pronouncements about Theistic Evolution.

The God Theory shows that evolution is a prevailing trend of **all creation**, not just biota, and that evolution is ultimately a product of the shaping influence of gravity (the "Hand of God, in motion") upon the universe. *The God Theory* is *primarily* concerned with the great flow of creation from the fires of the Big Bang to the appearance of modern ecosystems. Only in understanding this flow are we truly able to grasp our intimate connections to the Big Bang, and beyond. Only in attaining grasp of that **overall** flow is one truly able to discern the creative influence of the operative Hand-of-God in motion, and thereby preclude any need to debate Darwinism. That we are able to tie string theory to gravity, i.e. to God, means that we have gained actual evidence of the existence of God.

The notion that God unfolded the universe from a single event, via distinct physical processes, points to a calibration-of-calibrations (or as some might prefer a "miracle-of-miracles") that could not be produced by chance, in my opinion. That God was able to calibrate matter and energy into the precise mix needed to create our universe testifies to the greatness of His intellect and power. This is a new and exacting view of God, and one that is more profound than anything that can spin from a literal translation of Genesis, or from any facet of biblical literalism or fundamentalism. It tells us that the "miraculous" is only something that God is naturally capable of performing.

Composites of science and scripture help us to approach the truth, but the ultimate truths of the universe can only be rationalized within the context of a Just and Loving God—a God Who cares very deeply for His Creation. This brings *The God Theory* full-circle back to traditional theology and a major tenet of Calvinism—*that what God wants more than anything else is to be able connect with humanity.* We can see evidence of this throughout the scriptures. As Calvin noted, God seems to have given words (Divine Revelation) to the ancients that only formed "a shadow of an appearance of things" but by apprising man of the Divine reality, God built the bridge that would ultimately redeem humanity and lead us to the ultimate truths of the universe. That these truths are contained within the scriptures are illustrated by the "light correlation" discussed in Chapter Four, and by other profound messages of Genesis that need no further discussion. It is as if God gave us Divine Revelation specifically intending that it should occasionally jump out and smack us in the face!

Though science is a key to an understanding of Genesis, it is not the only key. On its own and in its strictest context, science is far from a witness to God. Pure science deals only with what can be seen, felt, touched, and measured, and with the weight of evidence at any one time. The Big Bang Theory, in a purely scientific context, only asserts that at a certain time, and under certain undefined circumstances, an explosion occurred which created our universe. While impressive evidence sustains the reality of that explosion and how it unleashed forces which have led to our being, the Big Bang Theory (on its own) says nothing about how and why the Big Bang occurred. The theory starts 10^{-46} seconds *after* the explosion began, not before. It says nothing about any universe that might have pre-existed our own. The anthropists (and others) have a completely different interpretation of the Big Bang, and reinforce their point of view with a philosophical device called "Occam's Razor" which allows them to rationalize the simplest explanation as the best, and therefore to "cut away" speculation about that which science inherently cannot measure. To them such an excision *must* be made, because there is no possible way that data can be obtained about what went on before the great explosion. Only by accepting the Bible enough to formulate a speculative "composite" of science and scripture is it possible to speak of such topics as the pre-creational universe, and the light correlation. However, pure science cannot condone such speculation. If we follow the path of pure science in addressing the greater mysteries of the universe we are left hanging desperately to the limb of paradox. Reason requires *The God Theory*.

I believe that *The God Theory* offers strong arguments in support of naturalism and theistic evolution. At the same time, I consider myself a scientist and a scientist always has a duty to be objective and point out the possible problems of any new idea. Thus, *The God Theory*'s greatest problems can be enumerated as follows: (1) it relies heavily upon circumstantial evidence, (2) it merges science and scripture into "composites," without proven rationale for doing so, and (3) it ultimately relies upon "string theory" to link the visible effects of gravity to God. Problems #1 and #2 are self-explanatory and need no discussion. In regard to problem #3, we must take note of the fact that the "Theory of Heterotic Strings" is far from proven, and far from complete. The prevalent and most widely-accepted theory of physics, describing the basic nature of the universe, is still the "Standard Model," with its emphasis on particles and particle theory. The basis of string theory is less well-established. Some physicists see it as a possible replacement for the Standard Model; others see it ultimately merging into the Standard Model. The problem in effecting either, at this time, is the tenuous nature of the theory. Heterotic strings have been conceptualized to exist at the incredibly tiny "Planck Scale" which is so small as to defy observation and analysis. Testing, therefore, has only been possible via mathematical modeling. This, however, has exposed a notable weakness of the theory—the fact that the universe *must* be composed of no less than *ten dimensions* in order for mathematical "workable hypotheses" to be able to avoid infinities (which innately refute the theory).

This, it seems, is a problem of significant magnitude. Hawking and other physicists have observed that a universe of more than three physical and one time dimensions would be inherently unstable.[52] Thus, some scientists reject the theory altogether and conclude that an "ultimate Grand Unification Theory" is not possible. Others believe that the dimensional problem has viable solutions, suggesting that perhaps the six surplus dimensions (that we cannot see or relate to in our universe) simply curled themselves up into tight, tiny circles and withered into the "Planck Scale" soon after the Big Bang (where they remain undetectable).

While the theory raises significant questions, it should be emphasized that the strongest advocates of string theory insist that the theory is far too powerful to be wrong. There is also a general consensus that the theory has marvelous order, structure and potential. The concept of "string tension," added by Scherk and Schwarz (the theory's co-founders) in 1974, has repeatedly allowed string theory to predict variations in gravitational power with precision. Some researchers now prefer it, in fact, to Einstein's gravitational theories. Subsequent work has also demonstrated that the theory accounts for other, hitherto inexplicable characteristics such as the innate "left-handedness" of certain particles, as noted by Hawking.[53] As far back as 1984, Schwarz and Green found that the "Theory of Superstrings":

> ...generated all the forces of nature, including gravity. Best of all, the substitution of strings for points eliminated many of the mathematical problems arising in other quantum gravity theories...[54]

The theory's greatest potential contributions are: (1) its solution of the gravity problem, and (2) its unification of relativity and quantum mechanics. Some take the "Standard Model" to implicitly suggest that at the smallest levels of the universe, the smallest of particles ultimately interconnect with a field that spans the entire universe. String theory may ultimately explain the nature of this field and thereby become integrated into the Standard Model. *It is therefore more than speculative. It possibly dovetails into the Standard Model.* The value of such contributions is potentially immense.

The *God Theory* thus steps forward as a theological tool designed to explain God, eternity and our being, leaving nothing out of the loop. At its essence, the theory asserts that the entire universe is interconnected (directly and indirectly) and that God is a product of that interconnection. It tells us that we are inevitably one, that the universe eternally oscillates between the alpha and the omega phases (of matter), and that this oscillatory process always occurs at a discrete and perpetually unchanging point in space, termed the "God-Point." Interestingly, it is also tells us that the Being and Persona of The Almighty came into being at this point in space, and implies that He reigns there, eternally. The *omnipotence, omniscience, and omnipresence* of God is an innate result of His interconnectedness to the pan-universal Heterotic string network. His *immutable*, unchanging attributes stem from His nature as a product of heterotic strings, which are implicitly the most basic and fundamental units of the universe. God is eternal because cosmic strings are eternal. God is the basis of everything because cosmic strings are the basis of everything.

So where do we go from here? We can only move in the direction of a theology that more accurately deals with the reigning God of this universe. God forbid that another religion, denomination or sect should be started based upon *The God Theory*. *The God Theory* is designed for universal application. It is a tool for linking theology to science and explaining the real God of the real universe. Perhaps more importantly, it explains why we can and should finally put away the Ptolemaic god of the Ptolemaic universe—a being who really has never existed. As John Calvin recognized more than four centuries ago, a primary objective of the Divine Plan is for God to engage us in an enduring relationship. To pursue that relationship, particularly during a new millennium in which "*our world*" is rapidly becoming "*our universe*," we must cultivate a new view of the grand scheme of things. A proper relationship with our God can only be built upon truth, and an intimate knowledge of Who and What God really is. The time for putting away superstition and ignorance is upon us.

The *God Theory* is now complete. The theory is based upon evidence, be it direct or circumstantial, scientific or scriptural, or all of the above. Before drawing this book to a close, I would like to offer some ideas that are simply that—ideas! The scriptures assert that we are God's creation, His children, His potential future companions in eternity. Yet, God is a very different sort of being than we are. The picture of God painted by this book, and by the

Bible, itself, is one of a spirit, a "virtual being," a persona Who exists within the "virtual realm" of the universe, Who by His very nature is eternal and unchanging. We who occupy the "material realm" of the universe have a very different framework of existence. Being innately composed of real particles of matter, we are here only temporarily. How then can we ever hope to enter the physical presence of God? A great gulf lies between God and man, the same gulf that separates the material from the virtual and the finite from the infinite. How can we ever hope to bridge such a gulf?

The answer is that we do not have to bridge it because everything in the universe has "symmetry." We, like the real particles of which we are composed, and the remainder of the universe innately have a "virtual side." Everything in the universe is a part of this dichotomy, this symmetry, and it is ultimately symmetry that cements all things to The Creator. God has given us a *virtual side so that a part of us will remain infinite and eternal, and never have to die.* The effect is to allow what we have traditionally called our *"immortal souls,"* to enter into an harmonious, perpetual, and fundamentally person-to-person co-existence with God.

Scientific philosophies like "anthropism" also hint of this duality and symmetry. Greenstein's description of the anthropic principle presented in Chapter Seven argues that ***"what is true of a single particle is also true of collections of particles: stones, planets— even the universe as a whole..."*** Because of symmetry, this argument implicitly *must* be extended to the ***virtual*** as well as ***material realms of creation,*** and we increasingly know that the universe is symmetrical. Furthermore, "virtual particles" are not fanciful creations. Science has proven their existence, just as surely as it has proven the existence of "real particles." So, there are really some strong reasons why we must assume that what is *generally* true of the real realm is also *generally* true of the virtual, a la Greenstein. As a result, we can suggest that the universe aggregates *virtual particles into virtual places, virtual things,* and even *VIRTUAL BEINGS.* Drawing this logic to its conclusion, if virtual particles are emitted whenever real particles interact, we can also expect the emission of

VIRTUAL BEINGS in response to the life processes internal to the physical body. Thus, when we cease to exist as physical beings, our bodies naturally emit our virtual being. An eternal relationship between God and His living creation is thereby maintained.

The notion of a transcendent real/virtual dichotomy within our universe may also solve other significant problems, including the problem of dimensions. Speculatively, if there are four dimensions in the material universe, then symmetry (and application of Greenstein's analogy) suggests that there are also *four virtual dimensions.* Interestingly enough, add four virtual and four real dimensions, and one obtains a total of eight. Add to these a dimension for *heaven* and another for *hell,* and suddenly we have a universe composed of ten dimensions—precisely as suggested by the Theory of Heterotic Strings. Another, more scientifically viable and rational way of dealing with the dimensional problem is to accept "tension" as a fifth dimension (the others being length, width, height, and time). Under the doctrine of symmetry we then come up with five dimensions in the virtual as well as material realms, for a total of ten.

Carrying supposition even farther—as real networks (the national highway network, for example) always have a single point of maximum centrality and connectivity, so does a universe composed of networks of cosmic strings. Indeed, as the national highway or air transportation networks also contain points of great *secondary* centrality and connectivity that are subordinate to the point of maximum centrality, perhaps the pan-universal string network contains similar subordinate points—subordinate to the "God Point." At the God Point, any note played by any cosmic string anywhere in the universe would be discernible. At lesser points, perhaps only part of the notes would be discernible. At the God Point all the information and all the power of the universe might be accessible. At lesser points only part of the power would be available because of inferior interconnections. Now here comes the punch line—if a persona that we call God came into being at the "God Point," what personas might come into being at the lesser points? Might the notion of lesser central places on a pan-universal string network explain the existence of a Gabriel, a Michael, or perhaps even a Lucifer? This tenuous and highly speculative line of thought, if somehow true, would resolve an ancient theological dilemma of how a perfect God could also have created evil and imperfection. The suggestion, here, is that He didn't create them, that moral forces like good and evil are simply natural products of a universe composed of networks of cosmic strings.

The major contribution of *The God Theory* will undoubtedly be its assertion that Almighty God came into being as a product of a network of cosmic strings that inherently spans the universe. I suspect that at some point in time, perhaps $10,000 \times 10^{10000}$ years ago, a network of cosmic strings began to play notes to a newly-awakening consciousness. These notes had, themselves, at some point in time, begun to fire across an inanimate network of cosmic strings simply because there was natural and inanimate movement in that network. Slowly, across vast and imponderable ages, in response to the stimuli of "tunes" being accidentally played by dancing strings, the network became *neural* and awakened. God stirred and slowly moved from the shadows and began to take control of the universe—a God Who *is* the universe, and its living consciousness. Before God, the universe did not exist, because without consciousness there is no existence and no universe (a la Greenstein, Chapter Seven). With the advent of the Divine Consciousness, eternity began, and the Great Caissons of Eternity began to roll perpetually between the Alpha and the Omega.

The fact that God became a consciousness, a being with a persona and a need for companionship, is precisely what led Him to change a deep, dark, cold, and hostile abyss—a pit filled only with mindless cosmic strings and empty space—into a vibrant universe of warmth, magnificent beauty and living, conscious creatures. God is the ultimate explanation and reason for all that has occurred! **What is so wonderful about this theory is that God, Himself, becomes the greatest of all miracles, and because of this we can more fully appreciate His existence and His accomplishments!!** God came forth from what we might describe as "nothingness" and saw the need for creation. In turn, he has given us *a place, a home, and a living existence*, where once there was only *a deep, cold, stifling, inanimate pit*!

If we accept the "light correlation," the many composites of science and scripture outlined in this book, and the ties between gravity (as an indicator of God's existence) and the persona of God, then we must also accept what the scriptures collectively and ultimately say about God. The essential message of scripture is that **He loves us and offers us an opportunity to spend eternity with Him,** *but He has just as clearly given us the freedom to choose the pit.*

God is a perpetual, eternal, caring, virtual being Who is a product of cosmic strings and the "God Point." It is instructive to compare such a deity with that rationalized by Frank Tipler's "Omega Point Theory," which envisions God as a more or less mechanical "information center" who essentially comes into being as the universe is collapsing into an "omega point" (from "Physics of Immortality").[55] Tipler's deity results from an accumulation of information at the omega point as the universe is collapsing. To Tipler, souls are simply stored bits of information about living beings, to be replayed, automatically, as the light cone collapses into the omega point. *The God Theory* provides a very different point of view, suggesting that God arose naturally at the "God Point" as a result of forces created naturally by an underlying, fundamental network of cosmic strings. God is not a passing artifact momentarily presiding over the universe at the time of its destruction; rather, God is the eternal, living universe and our implicit hope for the future. Within the *God Theory*, souls are not some passing relic to be replayed just before the universe winks out (a la Tipler); rather they are simply manifestations of the innate dichotomy of our real/virtual universe.

The God of the *God Theory* is a supreme intelligence Who emerged from nothingness, and Who is a part of everything. Conversely, everything is a part of Him. God does not exist in some shady aura of mysticism above a sphere of heavenly waters, perpetually gazing down on us from some detached and isolated heavenly throne, as medieval clerics believed. He exists in reality. He is real, and He is the ultimate basis and essence of the living universe, intimately tied to every part of it. In the words of the Psalmist:

Psalms 139: 7-12 (NIV)

7. Where can I go from your Spirit? Where can I flee from your presence?

8. If I go up to the heavens, you are there; if I make my bed in the depths, you are there.

9. If I rise on the wings of the dawn, if I settle on the far side of the sea,

10. even there your hand will guide me, your right hand will hold me fast.

11. If I say, 'Surely the darkness will hide me and the light become night around me,'

12. even the darkness will not be dark to you; the night will shine like the day, for darkness is as light to you.

The God of *The God Theory* finally becomes a deity just as real in the heights or depths of Mars, or on some planet circling a sun in a faraway galaxy as He is here. In truth, this is the God Who has been known to us for a very long time. He comes to us from the Psalmist, from the accepted scriptures and the unaccepted, from the east and the west, and finally He comes to us from science. We know Him from the words of people like Newton, Boyle, and Einstein, and we know Him from the words of prophets like Abraham, Moses, and Daniel. We know Him from poets who found Him in nature, and from commonfolk who have found Him in life.

He comes to us in *The God Theory* as the Alpha and the Omega, the beginning and the end, the first and the last, and the eternal. Though He is God of omnipotence and omniscience, He is also a living persona with a need for emotional companionship, and that explains our being. He is a God of Process Who creates by manipulating the forces of eternity, but He is also a God Who loves His Creation, and Who maintains our universe and our being, in part, because it is the preparation center and proving grounds for all who will be granted a perpetual companionship with Him in a realm where energy can neither be created nor destroyed, and where we as virtual beings may thus dwell eternally.

The God Theory tells us that God is real, that He is rational, and that He is filled with Divine Purpose. It tells us that just like any being, God prefers *a place* with beauty, warmth, life and vibrancy over the emptiness, the cold and the desolation of *an uncreated pit*. Yet, at the same time, it warns that the pit will be the final dwelling place of all those who are proven *unfit* to dwell eternally with the Grand Creator and Regulator of the universe. God offers us a marvelous and beautiful island of security in the chaotic seas of eternity, but we are free to swim those seas without His guidance, and drown.

My own journey through the *God Theory* has sustained my belief in the *overall* validity and accuracy of the Bible, while pinpointing significant scriptural, theological and philosophical problem areas! It has also highlighted the great need to adjust our prevailingly *ancient* theology to the greater truths of the real universe that we have found in science. This will be a daunting and perhaps even horrendous task, but it is not impossible. It will not be done in our lifetimes, but it will be done. In the composite of science and scripture there are visions of stunning beauty—a saga of how God came to be, of how He transformed something hostile into something intimately suited for life, of how He shaped creation and life, of how He continues to embrace, sustain and connect with all things, of Who and What He ultimately is and how He physically relates to us. Permit me a small adaptation of the prayer of St. Patrick to better illustrate this relationship:

God be with me, give me peace and harmony.
God within me, God around me,
God before me, God behind me,

God above me, God beneath me,
God on my right, God on my left,
God where I lie, God where I sit,
God where I stand, God where I am.
God all around me, through the galaxies, the universe,
God of creation, destruction, eternity,
God everywhere, and forever!

The universe that we discovered during the 20th Century is a naturalistic universe cris-crossed by pathways that lead inevitably to the doorstep of God. Naturalism is not a key to the door of "gnosticism" and disbelief, as some have claimed, instead it is the key to a temple of expanded faith and inspiration. It allows us to see the real universe while seeing the Real God. Yet, we must temper naturalism, and the theology of tomorrow, with knowledge that science can never be more than the way in. A "neo-natural theology" will not automatically place us on the foyer of The Almighty at the time of our death. It is our relationship with The Almighty, as spelled out in the scriptures, that provides the key to that foyer, and not everyone will be able to open the door. I can recall a candlelight service on Christmas Eve a few years ago—traditional hymns were sung, prayers were pronounced, scriptures were read, and as the service proceeded a unique aura of reverence fell across the congregation. My eyes were glued to the altar at the front-center of the sanctuary, and to those who came and went. Like everyone else, I sat quietly, meditative, focusing my thoughts on the events at hand. Suddenly, and for no precise reason that I can recall, I seemed to become aware *of something else* within the sanctuary! No more than two minutes after I became conscious of this presence, the pastor stood up and emphatically began a prayer with words: *"Lord, we are **CERTAIN** that you are here with us, tonight!..."*

I literally bolted upright in my seat. As he finished his prayer, it was as if I (a person perpetually unclean with sin) had been thrust into the presence of some burning, radiating goodness! The entire sanctuary seemed to grow warm, and took on a background-radiance that I could almost (but not quite) see. Thoughts of Moses rolled through my mind, and how he must have felt when He stepped into the presence of the burning bush! How marvelous yet disquieting it would have been for him to hear a voice emerging from that bush, a voice instructing him to remove his shoes because he was standing on hallowed ground! In the face of what I can only describe as my own contact with supreme perfection, I instantly became aware and ashamed of my own woeful imperfections! All I could do was pray a prayer asking for forgiveness that turned into a prayer of gratitude to a God whose wonders and magnificent perfection transcend the material universe, to a God whose majesty rolls forever between the Alpha and the Omega, and then back again. I could only thank The One Who gave me a place and a role in His eternal scheme of things, Who is perfect and Who demands the maximum possible perfection from me—yet The One Who is ultimately willing to tolerate my imperfections, to cleanse me and ultimately to bring me into His presence, forever.

As I look back now on the experience, I am reminded of a saying common to Jews, Christians and Moslems, alike, that *"God is great!"* This means exactly what it says, but it also means that God is living, loving, good, perfect, forgiving, and eternal. *It means that we live because of God's eternal love and greatness, and that because of His love there is eternal hope for us in spite of our imperfections.* All of this may seem miraculous, but it is actually just one more facet of God's perpetual rationality. **After all,** *we are His Creation, His potential future companions—children in search of a father, passengers on the great caissons of eternity!*

REFERENCES

[1] Nelson Inc., Thomas *The New Open Bible, King James Version*. Genesis 1:1.

[2] Robinson, John J. *Born in Blood: The Lost Secrets of Freemasonry*. New York: M. Evans & Company, 1989. p. 242-243.

[3] Spong, John Shelby. *Rescuing the Bible from Fundamentalism: A Bishop Rethinks the Meaning of Scripture*. San Francisco: Harper, 1991. p. 43-55—interpretation of the indicated pages.

[4] Same as above, p.53—direct quotation.

[5] Peacocke, A.R. *Creation and the World of Science*. Oxford, U.K.: Oxford University Press, 1979. p. 7.

[6] Gillispie, Charles Coulston. *Genesis and Geology*. Brockton, Mass.: Harvard University Press, 1951. p. 118.

[7] Peacocke, same as above, p. 7.

[8] Peacocke, p. 11.

[9] Jastrow, Robert W. *God and the Astronomers*. New York: W.W. Norton and Co., Inc., 1978. p. 11.

[10] Eddington, A.S. (from Stanley L. Jaki, *Cosmos and Creator*, Gateway Editions, Chicago, 1980), p. 56.

[11] Hawking, Stephen W. *A Brief History of Time*. 666 Fifth Ave.,

New York, N.Y. 10013: Bantam Books, 1988. p. 41.

[12] Jastrow, Robert. *God and the Astronomers*, p. 125.

[13] Hawking, Stephen W.. *A Brief History of Time*, p. 115.

[14] Nelson Inc., Thomas. *The New Open Bible*, Genesis 1:2.

[15] Sullivan, Walter. *Black Holes: The Edge of Space, The End of Time*. New York: Warner Books, 1980.

[16] Hawking Stephen. *A Brief History of Time*, p. 107.

[17] Same as above.

[18] Smith, Bradford. "New Eyes on the Universe," from National Geographic Magazine, Washington, D.C., January, 1994, p. 38.

[19] Smith, Bradford, Same as above, p. 38.

[20] Smith, Bradford, Same as above, p. 34.

[21] Rees, Martin. *Before the Beginning: Our Universe and Others*. New York, N.Y., Addison-Wesley, 1997. p. 182.

[22] "Official Super-Kamiokande Press Release" of Japanese physicists on June 5, 1998 (posted on internet from Takayama, Japan, at http://www.phys.hawaii.edu /~jgl/sk-release.html, 10/23/98)

[23] Jastrow, Robert. *God and the Astronomers*. New York: W.W. Norton & Co., Inc., 1978, p. 118-119.

[24] Greenstein, George. *The Symbiotic Universe: Life and Mind in the Cosmos* New York: William Morrow and Company,

1990. p. 130-131.

[25] Nelson Inc., Thomas. *The New Open Bible*, 2nd Peter 3:10.

[26] Nelson Inc., Thomas. *The New Open Bible*, Genesis 1:1-3.

[27] Reeves, Hubert. *Atoms of Silence: An Exploration of Cosmic Evolution*. Cambridge, Massachusetts: MIT Press, 1984. (original edition—Editions du seuil, Paris, France, 1981), p. 34.

[28] Greenstein, George. *The Symbiotic Universe*, p. 135.

[29] Sagan, Carl. *Cosmos*. New York: Random House Books, 1980. Copyright by Carl Sagan Productions, Inc., 1980. 246.

[30] King James Edition. *The Holy Bible*, Genesis 1:6.

[31] Sagan, Carl. *Cosmos*, p. 337.

[32] Reeves, Hubert. *Atoms of Silence*, p. 90-92.

[33] King James Edition. *The Holy Bible*, Genesis 2:4-6.

[34] Nelson Inc., Thomas. *The New Open Bible*, Genesis 1:9-10.

[35] King, Lester C. *Wandering Continents and Spreading Sea Floors on an Expanding Earth*. New York: John Wiley and Sons, 1983. p.1.

[36] Foster. *Historical Geology*, p. 128

[37] Strother, Paul (article "Pre-Metazoan Life" from "Evolution and the Fossil Record")

[38] Knoll, Andrew H. "End of the Proterozoic Eon," in *Scientific*

American, October 1991. p. 65-73.

[39] Schneider, Stephen H., and Randi Londer, *The Coevolution of Climate and Life*. San Francisco: Sierra Club Books, 1984. p. 15.

[40] Nelson Inc., Thomas. *The New Open Bible*, Genesis 1:11.

[41] Hawking, Stephen. *A Brief History of Time*, p. 127.

[42] Hawking, Stephen. *A Brief History of Time*, p. 125.

[43] Greenstein, George. *The Symbiotic Universe*, p. 135.

[44] Greenstein, George. *The Symbiotic Universe*, p. 223.

[45] Hawking, Stephen. *A Brief History of Time*, p. 55.

[46] Hawking, Stephen. *A Brief History of Time*, p. 122-123.

[47] Greenstein, George. *The Symbiotic Universe*, p. 158

[48] "Particle Metaphysics" in Scientific American, February 1994, p. 97.

[49] Paraphrased from Billy Graham, T.V. broadcast, 12-5-96.

[50] Hawking, Stephen. *Brief History of Time*, p. 68-69.

[51] Demarest, Bruce and Gordon R. Lewis, *Integrative Theology*. Grand Rapids, Mich.: Zondervan Publishing House, 1999. p. 43-45.

[52] Hawking, Stephen. *A Brief History of Time*, p. 164-165.

[53] Hawking, Stephen. *A Brief History of Time*, p. 161-163.

[54] "Particle Metaphysics" in Scientific American, February 1994, p. 97.

[55] Tipler, Frank. "Omega Point Theory," general summation

Printed in the United States
58853LVS00004B/107